GOD SPEAKS

Discover How He Communicates Through Dreams and Visions

Marilyn Scott

Gazelle
PRESS

Note from the editor:
For the privacy of certain individuals,
some names in this book have been changed.

ISBN 978-1-58169-414-7
For Worldwide Distribution
Printed in the U.S.A.

Gazelle Press
P.O. Box 191540 • Mobile, AL 36619
800-367-8203

To my children . . .
who have always encouraged, supported, and prayed for me.
May you always remember to let God use you in the gifts
that He has given you for His glory and honor, and remember to give Him the credit.

To my father and mother . . .
thank you for training me up in the way of the Lord so that
when I became older I would not depart from it.

In memory of my spiritual mother . . .
who is now deceased, and to my older living sister, whom
God used to teach me how to pray and not to be afraid to
pray with others, and who also taught me the wisdom in
being a praying woman of God.

Acknowledgments

To my heavenly Father, who is the Head of my life. If it wasn't for Him, I would not have these stories to share. I thank God for helping me to finally realize and understand my purpose in this life—to intercede for others and pray concerning things in our everyday lives. I thank God for helping me to work daily toward fulfilling His purpose for my life to reach my destiny that He had already planned for me before I was born.

This is something I prayed before I wrote each chapter after God led me to read Psalm 45:1. I took it and put it in my own words as a prayer to God. Here it is:

> Father, please let your voice and your tongue be my pen, for you have made me a ready writer.

To the many prayer partners and others, thank you for your prayers and support.

To my editors who took time out of your busy schedule to read my manuscript and provide feedback.

A special thank-you to my wonderful and handsome husband. It was you whom God used to inspire me to write and share what He put inside of me, which was being penned in a diary for many years, never realizing that He was going to take these stories to another level and have me share them worldwide, for His glory and honor. Thank you for your support. You have definitely been a strong tower for me to lean and depend on throughout this entire process. Love you!

—

Contents

And the Lord answered me, and said, Write the vision, and make it plain upon tables, that he may run that readeth it. For the vision is yet for an appointed time, but at the end it shall speak, and not lie: though it tarry, wait for it; because it will surely come, it will not tarry.

—Habakkuk 2:2-3

Introduction

When we get insight from God or God speaks, it's insight that is not limited to our circumstances today; it's beyond it; it's great insight; it's divine insight. When God speaks, He's giving us insight that we can't possibly comprehend on our own. That's why when we experience a dream or there's forecasting on something going on that tells us what it's going to be, we ask, "How can this be?" Well, it's because God can see down the road and we can't.

We don't understand what God is doing sometimes or why He's doing whatever He's doing, because we are looking at things from a natural realm, or should I say, from a natural time-and-space perspective. Therefore, we deal with things and interact during our time and space only in the natural. So we ask, "Why is this happening?" "What's really going on?" However, there's another realm called the spiritual realm where God's divine insight transcends time and space. In other words, the insight goes beyond and above what we see in the natural. This insight rises beyond the limits, or should I say, beyond ordinary limits.

Let me break it down. God looks at everything from beginning to end and all the processing in between. So His insight goes beyond the limitations of our perspective, present situations, views, and understanding. However, we are in time and space in the natural, and we're being developed through this time-and-space process.

God can and does speak to us from a spiritual standpoint and gives us guidance about who we are to become and what we are to do during the time and space He's given us. This can keep us from just existing, walking around like we are in "la la land" and spaced out, without a clue as to what we are to do with ourselves. Each of us is born for a reason, to do something, to be somebody, and to help somebody else. Only God can give us His divine insight and daily input about our life's journey.

God not only wants to speak to us through others but directly to us. He will sometimes do it through dreams and visions but not always. He speaks to us in various ways. He talks to us through songs, if we are really listening, and He can speak to us through instruments. His voice can be in waves of music; it's in the wind and the sea. They all hear and obey His voice, so why can't we?

God speaks to us during our personal quiet time; He speaks to us through the storms of life and in catastrophic events. God not only speaks to us in church gatherings, but He wants to talk to us anywhere, at any time, and through anybody or anything He chooses. He speaks to us through our children. He can even speak to some of us through our pets. He's spoken through animals before. God spoke to a prophet through a donkey so the angel with the sword would not kill the prophet. God let the donkey see the angel so the donkey could warn his rider that he was about to die if he took another step. Now that's supernatural!

I know God speaks to other people because I have heard many of you say He does. You have said, "I was about to go a certain way, and I heard a voice say to take a turn and go the other way" or, "Something told me to do so and so." But that could have been God directing you to get out of danger or for whatever reason, maybe He wanted you to see or meet a certain person. Let's give God more credit for how He directs our paths.

God desires to give us divine insight so we can understand and comprehend things that are about to take place that we will witness with the natural eye. We need to walk in the light and not in darkness so we can make godly decisions and pray about devastating things that are going to happen and ask Him to intervene.

If you are tired of making too many wrong decisions, tired of things happening around you and in your circumstances that you just don't understand, tired of not knowing why you are here and what God has chosen you to do, tired of not knowing whom to trust, tired of not understanding why things are revealed to you in dreams and visions that you just can't comprehend, I encourage you to read these true stories that are connected to divine insight through dreams, visions, and various methods that God uses to communicate to us, and to seek to know God through His Son, Jesus Christ. Seek to hear from Him, interact with Him, and respond by obeying Him. God will allow us to experience the supernatural.

1

A Wedding Planned in Heaven

Several years before I met my husband, Nate, I had a dream of meeting him for the first time:

> I was at a supermarket assisting an elderly lady with her shopping. I went outside the store and on my way to my car, I saw this young man and we began to talk.

In reality when I first met Nate, this dream didn't even come to mind; it was years later after we were married when God brought this dream back to me. I am sure it was when we were having some marital issues, and he was wondering if he had made the right decision about marrying me. He made it known to me then, of course; I did the obvious and wondered also. We were both in our forties, and sometimes getting married at this age can be quite challenging because we can be set in our ways while marriage is all about change. When we cross over from being single to married, there will be some definite changes to our lifestyle.

I have already shared the dream; now this is how it really happened. There was an elderly lady whom I occasionally called to check on to see if she needed to go grocery shopping because she did not drive. One day I dropped her off at the supermarket because she normally likes to take her time and get everything she needed to last her for quite some time. That particular day I had to go on a quick errand while she was shopping. By the time I returned, she was already at the counter, getting ready to check out.

She said, "Marilyn, I forgot to get some butter, can you please go and pick it up for me?" So I rushed to the back of the store to get the butter before the clerk finished checking her out. On my way to get the item, I noticed a young man and a little girl whom I thought was his daughter, only to find out later it was his granddaughter walking beside me as I hurried to get the item I needed.

As I was walking back to the counter, we just happened to meet up again and said hello to each other.

I said, "Your little girl's braids are so cute."

"Thank you," he said. "Don't I know you from somewhere?"

"I don't think so."

"I know I've seen you somewhere, or you look just like someone I went to school with."

"I've got to get to the counter and give Ms. Brown her butter because they've almost finished checking her out. I'll be right back."

After getting the item to the clerk, I went back to continue my conversation with the man.

He said, "You look just like a young lady I went to high school with." Then he mentioned her name.

"Maybe you saw me at a certain church that I attend." (I did not know at the time that he was a minister.) I mentioned the name of the church.

"Maybe that's where I saw you. I have visited there once or twice."

"When did you visit?"

After he told me the year he visited, I said, "Well, at that time I don't think I was regularly attending that church, but who knows? You may have seen me there, but I don't remember seeing you."

Then he began to share the names of some individuals that I knew.

I said, "Okay, yeah."

He then called out a few more names of people whom I really didn't know.

"I don't know them. Probably if I saw their faces, I would recognize them."

I couldn't talk with him much longer because it was time to take Ms. Brown home. Before I left he asked for my phone number, which at first I was really reluctant to give out. I had promised myself that I did not want to meet anyone else who was not introduced to me by someone I knew.

By the time I met Nate, I had really gotten tired of dating and getting into meaningless relationships. But I said to myself, *Well, he knows some of the same people I know from the church I attend so I can find out more about him from them.* I gave him my number, and I left to take Ms. Brown home.

The name of the supermarket where I met him in the dream was the same as the one where we met in reality, except at a different location. If I hadn't taken Ms. Brown shopping, I really don't know if I would have met him there because I didn't normally shop in that location. It happened just as I saw it in the dream—I was helping an elderly lady with her shopping when I met Nate. I can see it all just as if it were today. I know this is probably blowing somebody's mind—it blows my mind when I think about it.

God has His own reasons for putting two people together. Every time I think about how God reminded me that Nate and I were predestined to be together, I think about the story of Joseph and Mary's marriage. When Joseph found out Mary had already gotten pregnant before he took her as his wife, he was having some serious doubts and wanted to privately put her away. He knew that he was not the one who had gotten her pregnant. If this had taken place in today's world, I can imagine him saying, "You are what? Whoa, whoa, whoa! Wait a minute now, who is your baby's daddy?" So God had to send an angel to Joseph in a dream to tell him not to put Mary away because the baby that was conceived in her was of the Spirit of God, and he (Joseph) was going to be the baby's daddy and help raise him. Joseph accepted the circumstances because of the dream.

When Nate asked me to marry him, that same weekend I heard a voice say, "Call the television studio and ask the owner of a television network if you and Nate can get married there." I thought, *I can't ask him that because I haven't been to the studio in over a year.* (I had previously volunteered at the station, but after I moved several miles away, I hadn't volunteered for quite awhile.) When I was there I really didn't have much interaction with the office workers due to the fact that when I rushed into the studio, I went straight to the telephones. I was acquainted with a few people, however, and some of them may have been on staff. This thought stayed heavy on my mind all weekend until the following Monday morning when I went to work. I finally gave in and made the call and the receptionist answered.

"Hello, my name is Marilyn. I don't know if you remember me, but I used to volunteer there during the evenings."

"Of course I remember you, Marilyn."

I was very surprised that she knew who I was because I didn't recognize her name. So I said with a little reluctance, "Well, I'm engaged to be married, and we were making wedding plans and the thought of getting married at the studio came to me. I'm calling to ask John if we can use the studio to get married." Afraid of what she might say, I just stopped and paused for a moment.

She was so happy for me and with excitement she said, "Oh Marilyn, congratulations!"

"Thank you! I know it's a busy time, but this has been on my heart all weekend, even until this morning, and I had to call."

"I'll be happy to give your message to Amy and have her call you back. What is your phone number?"

"That will be great!" I said, then gave her my number and thanked her.

After I hung up the phone, I thought to myself, *I must be out of my mind. I can't believe I did that. O God, I pray that this is You leading me to do this.* I continued on with my work and gave it a few days before I called back.

When I followed up with Amy, I called and asked, "Hello, may I speak to Amy?"

"Yes, let me get her."

"Hello, this is Amy."

"Hi Amy, this is Marilyn."

"Oh yes, Marilyn, how are you? Congratulations on your

engagement! I heard about the good news. We have all been so busy around here. You know the next couple of weeks we will be having our Share-a-Gift, and we have been preparing for it. I understand that you want to get married at the studio?"

"Yes, the thought of getting married at the studio came to me. I wanted to ask John if we could get married there. I really hesitated to call because it's been awhile since I have been able to volunteer, and also I know the station is busy getting prepared for the Share-a-Gift."

"Let me talk to John and see what he says, and I will get back with you."

"Thank you, Amy. You have been so kind, and I really appreciate you taking the time to even check into this for me. I'll talk to you soon and say hello to John and Jane for me."

When I called Amy back the next day, I eagerly asked, "What did he say?"

"He said yes!"

"Oh my goodness! Thank you so much, Amy, for asking him, and be sure and thank him for me. I'll be getting back with you so we can work out the details."

"Great, Marilyn, I'll talk with you then."

Nate did not know about all of this, and I didn't want to mention it to him until I had more information. We had been talking about wedding plans and a date, but we did not have anything finalized. He had previously suggested we get married on April 1, and it took me about one-tenth of a second to reply, "No way, that's April Fool's Day! No way am I getting married on that day and that is *final!*" So that weekend we were discussing the plans because we knew it would be a small wedding. I finally told him that I had called the studio, and they had agreed to let us get married there.

He asked, "Are you crazy? There is no way we can afford to get married at that studio. It would cost thousands of dollars. Do you know how much it costs just for someone to get airtime on the station?"

"No."

"Well, it's got to be thousands of dollars an hour."

"Oh my goodness!"

"I think you need to call them back and find out how much it's going to cost because we may not be able to afford it."

"Okay. Nate, do you have a minister in mind to marry us?"

"Why don't you ask John to marry us since he's also a minister?"

Now I was looking at him like he was crazy. I said, "Nate, this man is very busy, and this is a very busy time for them. He's already said that we could get married at the studio, but I can't ask him to marry us, too."

"Why not? Just call and ask."

"Okay, okay, I'll call tomorrow and ask how much they are going to charge us and also if he can perform the wedding ceremony."

I really didn't want to ask John because I thought it was asking a bit too much. But since Nate's faith had kicked in, I said I'd better go ahead and do it. Maybe the same voice had spoken to him!

The next week I made another call and spoke with Amy and asked her to find out from John how much he would charge us for using the studio to get married and also if he would be open to performing the ceremony.

I couldn't believe I was asking him to marry us. He had already agreed to allow us time to get married in the studio.

Amy said, "Okay, I'll find out how much he will charge and also ask him if he can perform the wedding ceremony."

"Thank you so much, Amy, you are truly a blessing to us."

Amy called later and told me how much the charge would be for having the wedding in the studio—which worked for us—and also said John would be more than happy to perform the wedding ceremony.

Everything was happening so fast, and this was really blowing my mind. *Wow! Am I dreaming, let me pinch myself! Wake up, Marilyn! I can't believe all this is happening.* Well, by then I didn't know what to think, and I was just so excited and in awe at how things were working out that I took some vacation time off from my job, called the studio, and told them I wanted to come in and do a few hours of volunteering. When I later went to the studio to volunteer, I set up an appointment with John so that Nate and I could meet and talk with him since everything had been coordinated through Amy.

Nate and I had a meeting with John that night. Afterward the meeting, John took us to meet some of his staff and asked them to take a look at the programs to see where they could fit us in for the wedding. As they were going through the various programs, they decided to call a client who normally did his recording for his aired program at a certain time each week and ask him if he would be willing to allow John to perform a wedding during that time. They asked if he could switch and come in and do his recorded program at a different time. He rescheduled his recorded air time and allowed us to have the wedding ceremony. After all this was happening, I knew that the voice I had heard originally to call the studio was the voice of God, and I knew this was also the voice that told Nate to ask John to marry us. Everything was falling into place so well.

While we were at the studio, we were introduced to a young man who was on staff and also a musician. He asked us if we needed a musician, and I said, "Yes." So that night God blessed us with a time for the wedding and a musician.

The next day when I went to work, I suddenly had a desire for someone to sing at our wedding. Before the end of the workday I received a phone call from my cousin, with whom I had shared the exciting news. She told me that she had shared my wedding news with a friend, and this friend was so excited for me that she wanted to sing at my wedding. Her friend said she sang in a group, and she and the leader of the group could possibly do a song together. Then I shared with her that right before she called, I was just desiring that someone would sing at the wedding and wondering whom I could ask. I realized that I was experiencing the verse in the Bible that quotes, "*Delight thyself also in the LORD: and he shall give thee the desires of thine heart.*"

The amazing thing about this is that it just so happened that the young man was also the musician and a member of the same church as the television network owner, although Nate and I did not discover this until the day of the wedding. Well, the rest is history.

God used some very nice people to be a part of this wedding. We extend a special thanks to everyone whom God touched to be a part of what He had put together. The young lady who sang at our wedding also had the wedding videotaped and gave it to us as a wedding gift, which we watch on our wedding anniversaries.

I don't believe there is any marriage that does not have any disagreements or problems at some time or another. I truly believe that God puts couples together, and now I know personally that He gets involved in the wedding planning too. People say marriages aren't made in heaven, but I do believe this one was planned there. He had already spoken it in heaven, put everything together, and worked it out. As my spiritual mother would always say, "While we're trying to figure it out, God's already got it worked out!"

In this experience, God spoke to me and I listened, then responded in a positive way and so did Nate; and I am so glad we did. I know all this happened for more reasons than one. There are times when God speaks directly to our hearts. All we have to do is hope and pray that our ears are tuned in to Him and that our hearts are open to receive what we heard so we can respond and receive the blessing.

Planning weddings can sometimes be very stressful for the bride- and groom-to-be, with everything involved such as the expenses and the wedding party. There is usually a large checklist of things to be done in order for it to be a beautiful memorable day, which can be quite overwhelming. Then you have different people trying to give their opinions, and sometimes at the last minute someone just might get cold feet. I discovered that we need to be very sensitive to the voice of God all the way through the planning phase, up until the preacher announces, "I now pronounce you husband and wife." Yes, we need to still be listening for Him to speak because He is definitely still talking, but so is the devil.

However, we should seek God, first of all about whom we are to spend the rest of our lives with, and then include Him in the wedding plans. At the end of the day when the man and woman have said, "I do" to each other, the knot has been tied by only God, the man, and the woman. Therefore the results of a beautiful wedding and marriage can be based upon the couple consulting with God, the greatest wedding consultant and counselor, listening to Him, and following His instructions.

2

The Humbling Experience

The Break-Up

When Nate and I first were married, we had some issues, as most newlyweds do. Here we have two adults coming together in holy matrimony with different personalities under one roof. It's not like two people just making a decision to live together for convenience, to save on the bills, and if things don't work out, that's okay because they were just roommates. They could get all their things and go their separate ways since no godly covenant had been made. Marriages were not designed to work that way because marriage is a covenant between God, man, and woman.

Within the first few months of our marriage, we started having disagreements about things that escalated into a separation for a few months. I was so distraught and heartbroken, so as I prayed and fasted for God to bring Nate back home, I also asked, "God, where did he go—where is he?" One night the answer came in a dream—actually it was like an out-of-body experience.

I saw myself in the spirit inside a house. I was at the top of the ceiling looking down on some people who were talking. I vividly saw everyone in the room.

Months later when we did get back together, I decided to share the dream with him and described everyone I saw. Nate named every person whom I had seen in the room.

There is something else that happened while we were separated. One night we decided to meet for coffee, and I shared with him that I had a dream about him. In the dream God spoke to me and told me that he was being a Jonah. Then he shared with me that God had been dealing strongly with him also and told him that he was like Jonah, in the sense of being disobedient. I will never forget that night; the fear of God came over us, and I saw such a humble countenance on Nate's face.

Jonah had just flat-out refused to do something God had told him to do. He went on his merry way, thinking he could hide from the presence of God. He boarded a ship going to another city. God sent a great wind that caused their ship to almost be broken up, and when those on the ship confronted Jonah, he told them to throw him overboard. He knew he was the cause of their ship about to be wrecked because he was trying to flee from God's presence.

When they did, God allowed a big whale to swallow Jonah, and he was still alive and very conscious of what was going on while he was in the belly of this whale. He was in there for three entire days. The whale took him for a ride and it wasn't a joy ride, with the seaweed all around him, and I don't even want to imagine what else. I'm sure God and Jonah were having some very serious conversations during those three days. However, after three days of horror, Jonah was now ready to do whatever God told him to do.

God told Nate that he was running away from something that He had told him to do. I don't know what Nate's whale was, but he was there longer than Jonah. I'm sure just like Jonah, God and Nate were having some serious conversations because he decided to obey God too.

When we rebel against God's will, sometimes He will give us a "Jonah and the Whale" experience. Hopefully we will do as Jonah and Nate did and say, "Okay, Lord, I surrender." I know I've had quite a few of those and finally said, "Okay, I get the message." Sometimes He won't let us die in the whale, but He will have mercy and give us another chance to obey Him. God is a good and merciful God, and as I heard someone say, He's a God of another chance. I say, He's a God of many chances.

When I communicated to God my heart's desire to know where my husband had gone, He responded to me by revealing where he was by way of a dream. God is omnipresent—He's everywhere; therefore He knows where we all are. Even when we think we are hiding from each other, there is no hiding place from Him. Imagine that! He didn't only show me where my husband was, but He went a little further and said, "I will not only show you, but I'll take you to where he is." Now, that's supernatural!

The devil doesn't want us to get married because that's something that God ordained. During the dating period we can have an almost perfect relationship, but it seems the moment we tie that knot, that's when things will seem to start falling apart. All of a sudden we start running into people whom we used to date, or some old flings that we once had casual affairs with just start coming out of the woodwork—ones who we haven't seen in years. So now we have to tell them, "I'm married." They may get jealous because we didn't marry them and they may actually try to orchestrate a plan to break up our marriage.

It could go the other way: we run into someone we were once interested in, but they never showed any interest in us. We thought that they would never give us the time of day, but now they are letting us know that they want to get something going on. What are we going to do now! We are saying to ourselves, "Why now, why are they letting me know this now that I'm married, why did I have to run into this person now?" So we sort of say under our breath, "Uh, I'm married now," or we don't say anything at all. Well, did it ever occur to us that it could be a trap, a setup, a trick? Look at the timing. So we have to watch out for those traps.

As married couples, sometimes we get upset with one another, and we are tempted to talk to someone whom we know is interested in us or with someone with whom it seems that we can communicate better and end up confiding in them. However, we are failing to realize that they may agree with us for the simple reason that they don't think we should have married the person we are with anyway. They may even really believe our spouse is right in whatever the argument is, but they won't let us know. Therefore, this could be a huge problem and not always a wise thing to do.

Once a couple confided in me about their problems, and I encouraged them to communicate more with each other, to do more things together as a couple, and to pray together. If we can't seem to communicate with our mates, we can always pray and ask God to help us in that area; it's so important.

We should be our spouse's best friend. After all, our spouse is closer to us than anyone else, or should be anyway.

Another problem is finances, which some reports tell us is the number-one cause of divorces. Sometimes it seems like it's all three—sex, control, and money. Since reports tell us it's mostly finances, I'll touch on finances. Always, always be honest about finances with the person with whom you are going to marry. Then if they need to know something that could cause a problem after you get married, it will come out before you tie the knot.

It's better to have these discussions before the marriage so the two of you can agree on how to work out your finances together. I'm not saying there won't be disagreements because that's pretty well expected, but for the most part, you should work out what you can before marriage.

In today's society, most of the time, the man and woman have already incurred bills before they get married. This is a discussion to have only when you have made the wedding plans and are getting close to the wedding date and you know it's "fixin'" (Texas term) to happen. I don't believe anyone needs to know about your personal finances if you are not seriously in the planning stage of getting married; that's too much information to share. But if you are at the point where you are about to say, "I do," this may be something to consider. What if you get married and one of you just suddenly gets terminally ill or loses your job? The other one will have to take on the responsibility of handling the bills for the household until the sick or unemployed one gets better or finds a job. Unfortunately, there may be some surprises that you really don't want to know about, but you have no choice in the matter.

Nevertheless, I know this doesn't work for every marriage, and every couple has their own way of handling their household finances to make their marriage work. However, if something happens that will cause finances to become a major problem in the marriage to the point where it's almost causing a break-up, be willing to come together and pray about it so it can be worked out in a godly way. I am so glad that love can cover a multitude of faults.

Let's face it—men and women are different in many ways. Men sometimes think differently from women. It took me years to finally realize that and learn to accept my husband for who he is and how God made him. Now I realize he is just not going to be or think like me all the time. I am glad that Nate and I have different personalities because they actually balance the relationship; we help each other out in many ways. He has definitely helped me out.

We don't argue much; I can't say we never have disagreements, but as far as yelling at each other—we don't do that. It's always important for couples to have some prayer time together in addition to their own private prayer time. Nate and I always prayed together before we got married, and we continue to pray together today. I have found that when we keep prayer in our marriage, God will give us wisdom on how to have a godly and happy marriage.

So how in the world do two people come together with different personalities, backgrounds, cultures, dreams, and goals that they set for themselves before they even meet each other, to become ONE—that's a mystery within itself! God and only God can make us one. The Bible states that God took one of Adam's ribs and made Eve, and that a man shall leave his father and mother and shall cleave unto his wife and they shall be one flesh (signifying the togetherness in oneness).

There have been times when I was thinking something that Nate and I should do and was about to mention it to him and he took the words right out of my mouth. There have been times when God has shown us both dreams concerning the same thing. I always pray for God to make Nate and I one in the spirit so we can have the oneness that He meant for us to have in our relationship and in our marriage.

Yes, two become one and that's enough within itself to pray about. He said whosoever He had joined together let no man put asunder, and that means not even ourselves. Sometimes God won't let us take our marriage vows back even when we feel like taking them back.

An Angel at My Bed

I saw an angel appear at my bedside. The angel was a woman who was dressed in all white. She leaned over and whispered in my ear and said, "Nate is a man after God's own heart." Then she disappeared.

When I woke up, I wondered why she told me this. This was during a time when we were having some disagreements, and I was praying for him. Here I was thinking, *God, Nate needs to pray more and get closer to You.* We were having our different views about certain things, and I was thinking I was mostly right all the time—you know how it is. I was just praying, "God, Nate needs to be more humble, blah, blah, blah." But I was hit with a rude awakening. One morning I woke up about 4 a.m. and I had left the television on and praise and worship songs were playing. When I looked at the television screen a quote appeared, and it had something to do with being humble.

I remember saying, "God, yes!—that's it! Nate needs to be more humble and I'll tell him when he wakes up." Well, God busted my bubble. He spoke to me so clearly and said, "That was for you. If I wanted Nate to see it, I would have woken him up and brought him in the living room at 4:00 a.m. to speak to him." Wow, my face was cracked! I wish I had been in front of a mirror at that very moment to see my facial expression when that happened. What I learned was I needed to pray about keeping my mouth shut, and God would show me a more excellent way of how to be a wise and praying wife.

To say the least, I asked God to help me be more humble and help me to keep my mouth shut. I heard we should not pray for God to humble us, but I obviously needed to. God also told me that I was trying to get a speck out of my husband's eye when I needed to get the planks out of my own eyes so I could see my own imperfect ways. He reminded me that He knew Nate's heart better than I did, and He also knew mine.

Not only did God communicate to me in a dream about how He loved Nate and how He knew Nate's heart, but He also spoke directly to me. These have been very humbling experiences for both of us. Only God can give us wisdom in how to make our relationships better and stronger, in addition to us showering each other with love, gifts, and spending quality time with each other.

We have both learned that in order to continue to have a happy and godly relationship, we must go to God in prayer and listen to Him speak to us, whether He speaks directly to us or by using someone else so we won't be led to make an ungodly decision that we will regret later. I'm sure just as I was praying about Nate, he had also been praying about me and God answered his prayers. I think—I hope!

Whether we are in the dating stage and planning to get married or we've already tied the knot, God does not want us to exclude Him from the relationship-building process. He wants to get involved and teach us how to be better husbands and wives and how to live together as married couples. I believe He has already been trying to help most of us, but we didn't like what we were hearing, so we just disregarded His advice and made our own decisions. Or many times we listened to people who gave us wrong advice and we ended up making wrong decisions and terrible mistakes.

God created man and woman to come together and be united in marriage, which is a covenant He commanded (He ordained marriage), so who better to seek for wise counseling than God? He will also lead us to someone who will give us wisdom on how to create a good marriage. When things get hectic in our marriages, it's okay to go to Him and say, "Okay, God, I really need Your help because I'm afraid I'm about to mess up or have already messed up." However, we must be willing to listen, take His advice, and do what He says. We must leave it at that and feel good about the decision we made, knowing we made the best decision by going to God because He has the best advice.

3

The Battle of the Mind

I went to college thousands of miles away from home, and as I got closer to graduating, I decided to switch my courses and take them in the evenings so I could work during the day. But something happened during my last year of college as I was approaching my graduation date, and I almost experienced a nervous breakdown. I began to have serious migraine headaches, and sometimes I wasn't able to sleep at night. There was a young lady who came into the city and attended the same college; we became roommates and often prayed together.

One morning she said, "Marilyn, while you were sleeping last night, I woke up and saw a vision of a snake over your bed."

I said, "Oh my goodness, there is something terrible going on with me. I can't seem to sleep, and I'm having some excruciating headaches."

I walked to and from work, and one day as I was on my way home from work, I began to feel strange. I could feel myself walking as if I were out of control, sort of like in the form of a robot. Some way and somehow I would always make it to work and back home safely. But I knew something was not right. I don't know how I looked to others, but as I walked, it felt as if my body parts (especially my arms and legs) were moving in a robotic movement; then I knew Satan was trying to take over my mind and the battle for my mind began. I remembered when I was growing up, back home I would hear people say, "If the devil ever gets control of your mind, he's got you." That stayed with me, but I was determined that I was not going to let the devil take control of me. So I began to do the only thing I knew to do, which was to pray, "God, please, please don't let the devil take my mind." I cried and I prayed, then I cried and I prayed some more.

The church that I attended was within walking distance from where I worked, and the pastor's wife would conduct noon prayer meetings every day during the week. I would walk to church for noon prayer, and the pastor's wife would give me a ride back to work. One day I prayed so hard that I could feel large drops of sweat dripping down from my forehead. When I left prayer that day, I believed God was going to heal me.

I worked at a bank in the loan department, and my affliction was taking a toll on my productivity. It was taking me longer to balance the loans, even to the point that my supervisor took notice. She would come to my desk to see if I had balanced the loans before closing time. One day she came over to my desk and asked, "Marilyn, is there something I can do to help you?"

"No, I'm okay."

"I've noticed that it's taking you longer to balance the books, and you are normally very fast in balancing them. Are you feeling okay?"

"I'll be alright. I'm just going through something, but I'll be fine."

She knew something was not right because I always balanced the loans in a timely manner. My roommate started coming by the bank to wait for me so that we could walk home together. Sometimes she would have to wait for me longer than usual. Then one night I had this dream:

I was at church and a lady was standing up pointing at me and talking to me.

That was the end of the dream, and I could not hear what she was saying in the dream. Then about a week later, I went to church one night and I noticed there was a lady from another state visiting—she was the same lady I saw in my dream. I did not say anything to her; neither had I told anyone about the dream, but the following day I received a phone call from one of the members of the church who told me this lady wanted to see me. They told me where she was staying, so I went to visit her. Once I arrived she asked, "How are you doing?"

"I'm doing just fine."

"Come on in here, in the living room."

As we walked in the living room, she said, "God told me to send for you."

I was very nervous because I was wondering why she wanted to talk to me. As I sat down on the couch, she asked, "Is there anything bothering you? You look very weary. What's going on? God put you on my mind and said that I needed to talk to you. Don't be afraid. God is concerned about you and so am I."

I was reluctant to talk with her because I didn't know her; I had only seen her in a dream. She said, "Here, why don't you just have a seat and relax?"

As she began talking to me and trying to find out what was going on with me, I finally said, "I have been having some really bad headaches, and sometimes I find it hard to sleep. I feel like I'm losing my mind. Being here in college thousands of miles away from home, and trying to accomplish all my studies, and working on a job too, is beginning to feel too overwhelming."

As I continued talking to her, she said, "No wonder you are going to sleep in church. You are mentally drained. How are your eating habits?" God had obviously also revealed to her that I had not been eating right because at that point I had not mentioned to her that I had been having problems with my stomach also.

I said, "I fast a lot and I seem to have lost my appetite. My stomach hurts quite often." Actually when I wasn't fasting, I was hardly eating at all and I certainly wasn't eating healthy.

"What kind of foods are you eating? You have to start eating healthy foods. Why don't you stop fasting for a while and start nurturing your body back to health? Start drinking milk to help heal your stomach." She suggested other foods I needed to start eating and advised me to stop eating foods that were not healthy for me at that time.

She told me something that I will never forget and still follow to this day. She said, "If things ever get so bad that you need to talk to someone, always ask God to give you at least one person that you can confide in and pray with and never hold things inside to yourself."

She suggested that I rest for a few minutes, then she prayed for me before I left. I took her advice and started trying to eat healthier foods.

Sometimes it's hard to find a person you can trust to talk with and confide in. I have learned that we just have to let people know, "Please keep this confidential," because sometimes they may not know we don't want others to know unless we make it very clear. Pray that God sends you to someone who is not a spy, a gossiper, a busybody, a traitor, or just downright nosy, but someone who is sincere in wanting to see God work things out for you. Many people have been hurt by telling someone something that was supposed to be confidential, and it got out when they knew they only told one person, so we all have to be careful. I once had a pastor who, at the end of the benediction at church, would have everyone say, "Lord, keep my tongue." I have to continuously say that prayer even to this day.

The following Monday morning after my visit with that lady, I went to work and I knew that God had healed my mind because I had been sleeping very well. I felt like I was back to normal, and I was no longer walking like I was completely out of control. As I was in the office sitting at my desk, one of the loan officers in my department walked by me and said, "Well, at least you are not talking to yourself anymore," and expressed happiness for me.

I looked up at him surprised at what he said, smiled, and then thought to myself, *You mean that I had been talking to myself and didn't even know? No one ever pulled me aside and told me I was talking to myself or that I was talking to myself in an abnormal way.* To think about it, at some time or another, some of us do talk to ourselves. But how many people do we see and hear talking to themselves and say to them, "Hey, do you know that you are talking to yourself?" Think about it. This man let me know that he and others in the office knew that I was experiencing some serious issues. When he said that, I knew that someone else had noticed that something miraculous had happened to me over the weekend.

When I think about the lady that God sent to pray for my healing, it reminds me of a story in the Bible when God blinded a man name Paul (whose name was Saul at the time). God spoke to a man named Ananias in a vision and told him to go and find a man who was called Saul. God told Ananias that Saul was now a praying man; and in a vision He had also shown Saul that a man named Ananias was coming to pray for him that he might receive his sight. Ananias obeyed God and went and found Saul to let him know that God had sent him to pray for him to receive his sight, and Saul was immediately healed.

God immediately healed my mind after the lady prayed for me. Who knows, this lady may have seen me in a vision too. I don't know, but what I do know is that I saw her in a dream, and God also spoke to her and told her to send for me and pray with me and I was healed.

I was really ready to go back home to Texas after that battle, so I decided to take some summer classes to finish up college sooner. God blessed me to complete all my courses and I graduated shortly thereafter and moved back to Texas. When I went back, I was able to get a very good job at another bank also in the loan department, which was a promotion for me.

After that battle, I felt I could understand some of the things some people may have experienced when they were on the verge of having a nervous breakdown or eventually experienced one. Experiencing a nervous breakdown is a very devastating thing; it's a battle and when it starts to happen, if we don't realize what's going on, this evil spirit could take over the mind and control it. It's an evil spirit because it destroys the mind to the point where people can't function or even think normally. I have a lot of compassion for people who suffer with mental illnesses, and when I see them, I pray for them that God will heal them.

I thank God and rejoice for His restoring my mind because it was definitely a battle of the mind. I learned from this experience that God can heal our minds. God spoke to me one day and said, "I delivered you and restored your mind, now I want you to pray for the minds of the people. I healed you and I can heal others." I now realize that God took me through that battle so I would personally know that if anyone becomes afflicted with mental issues, He can heal them.

There are so many people with mental problems, and they aren't all in mental institutions or hospitals. We have heard of people who just snapped while at work, at home with family members and friends, or walking the streets, and some appeared to be normal. There are all kinds of mental illnesses, and not all of them are the same. A person doesn't have to walk around looking crazy as if they have lost their mind to be having mental issues; they can look perfectly normal without anyone detecting that there is something strange going on with them; but inside that mind, all kinds of things can be going wrong. We should also be careful what we let enter into our minds, what we watch on the big screens, and what music and songs we listen to—just as we become what we eat, we also can become what we let enter into our eyes, ears, and minds.

Many people may not even realize what's going on with them when they begin to experience some sort of mental changes, so if people don't know, many times they won't get the help they need. But if we see this happening to someone who is close to us, or if we notice a change in their normal character, we should see if they need help and definitely pray for them.

Haven't you ever heard of other stories like the one in this scenario?

> Someone started to notice little things concerning a person's mental state. They mentioned to others, "Have you noticed so and so has been acting kind of strange lately? I wonder what's wrong." As they began to closely watch them every day, that person's state of mind progressively grew worse and then they noticed that person was no longer at work. Then someone asked, "What happened to so and so?" and someone answered, "Well, I heard they eventually had to be admitted to a mental institution," and everyone said, "Wow, they're in my prayers."

Since I've experienced this, if I ever see someone whom I'm close to or know personally climbing into a shell, I begin to first pray for them. I pray for guidance as to how to go to them and show concern. I realize that not every person will be receptive to someone coming to them with concern when they are experiencing mental issues, so I would pray and ask God for wisdom on how to approach them. People have different mental issues, and the results may not always come out the way we hope; therefore, this is something to be very careful and very prayerful about. Also, when I see people with mental issues and I don't know them personally, I still pray for them that God will heal them as He did me.

God healed me and would not let the devil take my mind, and I am so glad that I had the faith to believe that He could heal me. I encourage you, if you ever feel so stressed out that it begins to take a toll on your way of thinking, or if you begin to experience things that are affecting you mentally, please tell someone whom you trust about what you are feeling or experiencing so you can receive some help. There are hot lines, clinics, doctors, and ministries available to help people who feel like they are experiencing these kinds of symptoms.

I also encourage you that when it seems like you can't get a prayer through, ask God to help you get in touch with someone who can pray with and for you. I am so glad that God sent me a roommate who believed in prayer, who believed that God would answer our prayers, and who was not afraid to pray with me. He will give you peace in your mind, and when people look at you knowing what you just went through, they will know it was God who worked a miracle in your life. We can't see God working in the spiritual realm using His powers to work miracles in our lives, but what we can see with our natural eyes are the results of His miraculous powers.

When I look back and think about how I saw the lady in a dream pointing at me, which signified she was talking to me, I realize that God was letting me know that He was making a way for me. The dream also let me know that before I even met this lady, in the spiritual realm God saw me, saw that I needed help, and was concerned so He gave her a message for me. He communicated with her by some means that He wanted her to pray for me and talk to me because He wanted to heal me.

So I was on the receiving end of someone contacting me and telling me that God spoke to them and told them to contact me. I am so thankful that this lady paid attention; she saw me while I was in church and she obviously saw something else going on concerning me that made her be concerned about me. I've fallen asleep or have gotten sleepy in church before many times, and no one ever seemed to have been that worried until she did that day.

I've seen other people fall asleep in church, but that doesn't mean something is wrong except for the fact that they may be fatigued. Perhaps they went home from work, prepared dinner for their family, took the children to their extracurricular activities, and went back home to get dressed for services; or it could have been that they were sleepy from side effects of medication. Some people suffer from insomnia and have a hard time sleeping when they go to bed, so when it does hit them, wherever they are, they have to fight to stay awake if it's not an appropriate place for them to be sleeping.

There are various reasons people fall asleep in church; it does happen at times, but I really don't believe people intentionally go to church to sleep. One reason that I could have been falling asleep in church was that I couldn't fall asleep when I went to bed at night. To say the least, I don't have any problems sleeping now, neither have I had those excruciating migraine headaches. As for being fatigued, I've since learned to eat healthy meals, take vitamins, and make sure I take some source of iron.

But the point is, normally we don't contact people just because they get sleepy and fall asleep in church. There has to be something else that we sense going on with them, something we see or that God lets us know is going on with them. This lady told me that God told her to send for me. She responded to God, and more than likely I would have never even approached her and let her know that I dreamed about her, so God knew He had to have her contact me.

I am thankful to God that He loves us so much that He wants to heal us. He didn't have to use this lady to bring about my healing; He could have just healed me without her even being involved. I love the way God works in our lives by using us to help one another. I love the way He communicates with us, but we must have faith in Him, pay attention to Him, learn how to listen to Him, be sincere, respond to Him, and be willing to obey Him. It does not only benefit others, but it can also be beneficial to us as we see His wonderful and miraculous works performed.

When God speaks to us concerning the state of mind of an individual, it's imperative that we pay close attention to what He is saying. The information and instructions He's conveying to us are important, and if we aren't sure what actions to take in situations like these, we should ask Him to direct us to someone who is professionally trained on how to handle these types of conditions because they are case-sensitive. But know that when He comes to us, it means He is concerned about this person and wants to see them healed. Listen and respond, so that a mind can be healed.

4

The Heavenly Shoes

There are three women who mentored me on how to become a praying woman, and I've learned valuable lessons from each of them. They not only taught me how to be a praying woman, but about the power of a praying woman.

One of those women was my spiritual mother, who is now deceased. If you knew Mother Mary, you know that she loved to wear beautiful, stylish shoes. She was an evangelist and had the anointing of God on her life. God used her to pray and prophesy into the lives of many people. She would always say, "Just call me Evangelist or Mother." She was known and still is known as one of the most anointed prayer warriors of all times. I was blessed to travel with her and accompany her during some of the citywide prayer revivals she held. Have you ever sat down and listened to an elderly person as they spoke and words of wisdom came flowing out of their mouths in such powerful and God-given advice? That's the way Mother Mary was.

I believe if we listen to the wise elderly and seasoned men and women, some of our lives and homes would be in better condition, and there would be more respect in the home for each other, from the man or woman of the house all the way down to the children. Mother Mary mentored, trained, and taught women how to be women of God, how to be women of the home, how to treat and respect our spouses (she didn't leave the men out), and how to take care of our children.

I remember I had gotten tired of being embarrassed by the shameful way I had been living. I had just started going back to church, and I asked my pastor at the time if he knew of a seasoned woman of God by whom I could be mentored. The man of God immediately called Mother Mary, and after speaking with her, we connected and she began to mentor me. I traveled with her as she conducted revivals, and I learned so much just sitting under her teachings. Mother Mary had a heart for helping pastors, and she would always conduct revivals for them. I remember asking her why she didn't go to the megachurches, and she said that God had given her a burden to help the pastors of smaller churches— to undergird them and stand in the gap for them. There are people put in certain places for various God-given reasons, and we have to pray and ask God where our place is to be effective in that place.

I would listen to her give wise counsel to people concerning their spouses, and she would say, "God loves them and they're in the hands of God." And if one or the other spouse seemed to be getting out of hand and going contrary to the ways of God or mistreating the other spouse, one of her favorite quotes was, "Don't you worry about them, they ain't running nothing and the devil ain't either." That quote always gives me peace and confidence in knowing that whatever oppositions I have to face concerning anything that the devil brings against me, I shouldn't worry because God is in total control of every situation. I learned a very valuable lesson from Mother Mary: we should always see the good in our spouses and encourage each other because none of us are perfect until God makes us perfect. We all have faults, whether we want to admit them or not, and God has to constantly remind us of this.

Mother Mary always said, "Don't put your mouth on the man or woman of God." She told me if I saw them doing something that was against God's will to just pray for them. She said, "I've witnessed people who died for saying things against the servants of God, and it's a very dangerous thing." As long as I knew her, she always kept a positive attitude about people. She would say to me, "Let's pray for them." She would say that there were people who had died premature deaths because they had talked against or slandered a man or woman of God in a way that was not pleasing to Him.

I experienced such an encounter, which frightened me, and I will never forget it. I knew a woman of God who was quite younger than me and she had some issues, as we all do. One day while I was visiting one of my sisters, this woman called her while I was there, and I was having one of my real sassy moments. I was being sassy and saying some things I should not have said concerning her. Then I left my sister's house and was on my way home.

I had dropped my husband off at the golf course, so on the way home I had to stop and pick him up, and I just happened to look up in the rearview mirror and noticed that there was a spot on my forehead. It was not hurting me, so I didn't even know it was there. As I continued to look at it, it looked to be swelling and getting even larger. It was not from

a mosquito bite, and I knew I had not hit my head on anything or even felt any kind of sting or pain, but it was getting
larger and I became really afraid.

I heard the voice of God say, "Repent for talking about
this woman of God. You could have an aneurysm right now."
I began to repent and ask God to please forgive me for
talking about her and to heal me of whatever had suddenly
come upon me. I looked in the mirror, and the spot immediately disappeared.

God said to me that this woman was sick unto death, and
she had been through some very hard times in life. He told
me to pray for her because that could have been me in that
predicament. She was admitted to the hospital, and God
dealt with me and told me to go to visit her and pray with
her. I'm sure you can imagine how I felt. Even though the
thing that I was saying might have been true, in God's sight,
it made Him angry with me. This was a lesson and a very
true awakening that I will never forget. Even now there are
times when I'm tempted to say certain things about someone,
whether they are a Christian or not, but I stop and think
about what happened to me on that day and I pray and ask
God to keep my heart and quiet my tongue. I try to always
remember to say this scripture every day:

> *Let the words of my mouth, and the meditation of my
> heart, be acceptable in thy sight, O Lord, my strength, and
> my redeemer* (Psalm 19:14).

God really put His fear in me and humbled me that day,
and I am glad He spared my life. Weeks later this young lady
died. I was reminded of how God wants us to have compassion for others and reach out to give a helping hand instead

of dwelling on their past and their weaknesses, especially if they have changed for the better. We are to pray for one another and hold one another up because at some point in this life, every now and then we all struggle with some kind of issue.

Today, I am glad I had that encounter with God. I am a witness and a firm believer that sometimes when bad things happen to us, we don't always consider if we have hurt someone with the words that came out of our mouth—whether direct or indirect—whether true or false.

So I've learned to be very careful of how I treat others. When we maliciously try to hurt someone or talk bad about someone, God is listening to what we are saying, and when He isn't pleased with our actions, He may let us know it in some way or another. Therefore, I experienced exactly what Mother Mary was telling me when she said, "Be careful what you say about God's children," and I know firsthand that can be dangerous.

"Wow! What Beautiful Shoes!"

However, back to Mother Mary and those beautiful, stylish shoes that she loved to wear. She always dressed like a queen from head to toe. To me she lived like a queen—her home was very beautiful and elegant, and everyone was always welcome there. It was so peaceful because she always, always prayed and held many prayer meetings in her home. Many people would call her for prayer, and I never saw her turn anyone away, no matter what time it was. Later in life she became very ill and one night I had a dream about her.

I saw her walking in a pair of the most beautiful sparkling and shining shoes. I saw her actually walking in what I would call the firmament, which I thought to be heaven.

I shared the dream with her and I would hear her say, "Marilyn say she saw me walking in some beautiful shoes in the heavenlies," and she would be so happy. Years passed and she went home to be with the Lord, but before the Lord took her home, I believe that God was letting me know that He was going to take her home to be with Him and in heaven she would be healed. He had some of the most beautiful heavenly shoes waiting there just for her because that's what she loved. I can still see her walking in the heavenlies in those beautiful, sparkling shoes even today! Wow, what a blessing!

Is there anything down here on earth that you would like to have in heaven? Maybe it's a hobby? Can you imagine God saying, "I have plenty of that (whatever it is) for you in heaven, in your heavenly mansion"? Maybe you like playing golf like my husband does; in heaven it never gets dark, the weather is always a perfect golf day with no wind blowing (maybe slightly), all those nicely kept fairways and greens and a few sand traps every now and then, maybe a few water holes but not too many so the game won't be frustrating, but a little challenging. And here's the kicker: custom-made golf clubs just for you (lots of them).

However, if it were true, just thinking about it should make some of you golfers want to go to heaven, if golf was in heaven. Somebody is probably saying it would be nice to have an eighteen-hole golf course in the back of their mansion or at least a golf course with nine holes, and a chipping and putting green. But I love crystal and I can imagine me with a crystal home, crystal windows in unimaginable beautiful colors, and several crystal items in my home. Wow! Now that would be something to behold! I hope so—just a thought.

Think about it a moment, whatever you like collecting, wearing, doing for a hobby that is acceptable in God's sight— that may be there waiting for you in heaven. God has many things that He wants to talk to us about. He not only talks to us about getting to know Him and His Son, Jesus Christ, and having that intimate relationship with Him, but He talks to us about things we can enjoy while we're here on earth.

He will give us the desires of our hearts, and I believe He may even give us some of our heart's desires when we get to heaven, but the difference is that when we get to heaven our eyes will not have seen, our ears will not have heard, and neither has it entered into our hearts the things He has in store for us. Now that's enough to look forward to that heavenly place just to see what He has waiting for us.

God revealed to me that Mother Mary is wearing some really beautiful, stylish shoes, and I guarantee you they are some of the most beautiful shoes she has ever worn. Now I'm not saying that your heart's desires will be there—but IMAGINE THAT!

Obviously He wanted me to share this dream with her because she was still living when I had it. I'm glad I did because her face just lit up, and she began to glow and smile and would often share it with others. I'm sure she was imagining how beautiful those shoes were going to be in heaven. I'm sure she felt as if she could not wait to get to heaven to receive her gift and see the most beautiful shoes she had ever seen. Now that is what I call having so much favor with God that He reveals He has a gift waiting in heaven just for you. Doesn't it make you wonder what other great surprises He has waiting?

I am so happy that I had the opportunity to see such beauty and that I obeyed God's voice when He said, "Now share it with her." When we not only see the wonderful images in our dreams, but afterward we listen as God tells us to share what we saw with others, we can witness the joy and happiness it brings to their hearts.

5

The NFL Player

Our sons have played football since they were very young and participated in Little League football teams. They were blessed to receive both academic and athletic scholarships, which helped them to further their education and achieve their degrees. Our youngest son was blessed to be named SWAC Newcomer of the Week during his freshman football year and later made the All-American first team as a running back playing for a Historical Black University (HBCU). After receiving his degree, he went on to participate at the professional football level in NFL camps.

Nate played football in high school, in semi-pro, and he also tried out for kicker and safety at a couple of NFL camps. He got hurt with a knee injury, which ended his football career, and as a result Nate took up playing golf. Therefore, I know a little about football and have always enjoyed going to the games and watching them on television. So you know there's a lot of football watching in our house with my husband and our sons.

However, one day I heard a voice say to pray for a particular professional NFL player. I did not know much about him except for watching him play football on television, and I would hear my husband say how great a football player he was. I heard the voice again say, "Pray for him." I finally got concerned and thought, *Why does this young man's name keep coming to me to pray for him?* So I began to pray for him. I really didn't know what to pray about, so I would pray for the normal things such as his protection, help in his football career, his salvation, and whatever else God would lead me to pray about.

Several years passed and I finally found out the reason I was praying for him. I have learned that when God burdens my heart to pray for someone, I should just do it! In fact, years after this, I saw him and had several opportunities to let him know God had me intercede for him, but I did not feel that it was the right time. I remember once when Nate and I walked right by him and he overheard us talking and saying little sweet things to each other, he said, "Yuck, listen to them with all that 'baby' this and 'honey' that stuff, you two are making me sick." Then everyone just burst out laughing. We told him we thought he was a great football player and that we were praying for him as he went to his car.

I still pray for him and his family because I truly believe he has a special calling on his life, and God is using him in His own way. I also believe God is going to take him to a deeper depth and a higher level of an intimate relationship with Him. In these past few years, God has also added another NFL player to the list for me to say a special prayer for him and his family. Again, I don't know why and I don't have to know all the details, but I've learned to be obedient to God and pray. God is so mindful of us that He will always have someone praying for us. You know, we don't know who God has praying for us, but thankfully He puts us on someone's mind and tells them to pray.

There may be people who believe God doesn't care about athletes or the sports they play. In Bible days, Paul always talked about the prize of the game as being the ultimate goal, which lets us know that for centuries sports have been in existence, even in ancient times. God loves a person who plays sports for a living just as much as He loves a person who sits behind a desk, works as a manufacturer, in the ministry, or any other occupation. God can use us in whatever career or field in which we believe we were born to work. People who are in sports careers need encouragement, love, and prayer too. They have families, friends, and fans whom I'm sure are concerned about their livelihood and health, as well.

It looks like a lot of fun and excitement to us as we watch them huddle up and get ready to get banged and beat up. However, unless we live with them or are in their football uniforms out there on that field, we don't know about the suffering they deal with, especially from the hits they take, and we certainly can't feel the pain they have to endure on and off the field. As I think about it, I have never heard a football player, while he's being interviewed, complain and constantly harp about the excruciating pain that comes with the job. They just get out there on that field all hyped up and ready to go to work.

As a dreamer, I believe one of the most effective responses we must take is to pray and also find out from God how to or if we need to relay any messages. I believe, if you haven't already experienced this yet or discovered it, you will notice that you have not only been receiving messages through dreams, but there have been times when you heard a voice say, "Pray for someone or about something." I'm sure you have experienced this; you know how we say, "Something told me to say a prayer for . . ."

There are times when God will tell me to contact a person and pray with them, and other times He just says to pray for them. James, Jesus' brother, encouraged us to pray for one another; prayer changes situations and people.

I can remember the very first time I heard that voice, say, "Pray for him." I did question the voice when I first heard it, inquiring and wondering why. This person was a concern to God, concern enough to put him on someone's mind. I believe God even had other people praying for him who were, as I was, not even in his inner circle, not close to him, who really knew nothing about him, and maybe, as it was for me, the only time I really paid any attention to his name was when my husband would say he played great ball.

Sometimes it's not always about contacting the person, but it is always about praying for them. I am thankful that I didn't brush it off when God told me to pray for him. It did encourage me to be more attentive to that small, still voice when God revealed to me the reason He had me praying. We can miss the opportunity of saying a special prayer for someone if we just brush it off when we hear that voice. What I've discovered is that we often are too busy, get distracted, and forget. I encourage you that when you hear that voice to respond by whispering a little prayer.

6

"I Saw Death Upon You"

I always dream about certain families if there is going to be a death in that family—before it happens. I have gotten to the place that when I have these dreams I immediately go into prayer. Many times God does not show me a specific person, but He does identify the family. I remember the morning when I frantically was awakened from this dream:

My husband's family members were attending a funeral. We had all gathered in the church and were sitting in the front pews, then we started to walk around to view the body; however, I did not see the person who was in the casket.

That was the end of the dream. I wondered if maybe I had the dream because, subconsciously, Nate's parents' passing could have still been on my mind, because he had just lost them both on the same day within at least fifteen minutes apart a few months earlier. In the dream, as I was walking to the casket, I was standing next to one of his siblings, and since I didn't see Nate standing next to me, obviously I thought the worst when I woke up so I began to pray for him.

I continued to feel a heavy burden on my heart, as if something could happen suddenly and very soon. Knowing how God deals with me, I was reminded that sometimes God shows me a person but the dream could be about someone close to them. I began to pray all morning long, "God, please spare this person's life, please don't take them, and please don't let there be another funeral in this family this soon."

That same morning my husband and I decided to go golfing. Most of the time we have prayer together before we walk out the door, and I continued silently in prayer for his family as we were going to the golf course. While we were playing a round of golf, Nate received a phone call from one of his brothers informing him that their brother had fallen about eighteen to twenty feet and landed on solid concrete at his job. He had to be rushed to the hospital. When we got to the hospital, his brother was in serious condition with rods and screws visibly sticking out of both pelvises, and with a plate in one of his arms. He was in intensive care and could not move.

I had not mentioned the dream to my husband before we left to go golfing, because I didn't want him to be worried. If you know anything about serious golfers, one thing you don't want to do is mess up their concentration. I didn't mention the dream to him on the way to the hospital either. Later that day, I finally shared with him how I woke up with a heavy burden for his family and had been praying all morning.

Thank God, his brother is healed today after going through surgery, being in a wheelchair, and working through therapy for several months. I know we could have had another funeral if the Lord had not intervened, spared his life, and healed him.

"You Were in a Casket"

I recall when I was in my early twenties, I had a dream about one of my sisters.

I saw her in a casket and I was looking down on her.

I woke up in the middle of the night frightened and wanting to call her immediately, but it was too early. I had to wait because I didn't want to frighten anyone by calling so early in the morning and telling them what I had just seen. So when I finally did call, I shared the dream with her. She shared with me that someone had threatened her life, but she was alright. I told her that I had been praying all morning long. That's been so many years ago, and my sister and I still talk about how God has spared both our lives and how merciful He is.

There is a story in the Bible found in 2 Kings 20 about a man name Hezekiah who had become sick unto death. He was given a message by a prophet of God. God said for him to get his house in order and his soul right with God because he was going to die. But Hezekiah wasn't ready to die, and he pleaded and cried for God to spare his life. God spoke to the prophet Isaiah and told him to tell Hezekiah that He had heard his prayer and seen his tears and that He was going to heal him. Hezekiah was told to go to the house of the Lord. God told him that He was going to add fifteen years to his life.

There are times when death comes knocking at our door,

but if we communicate with God and talk to Him, He might be gracious and merciful unto us and give us some more years and time to get our house in order and our life right with Him, if we haven't already. God is so merciful that He does sometimes allow people time to repent before He calls them home because it is not His will that anyone should perish. He sent His Son, Jesus Christ, so that we could have eternal life.

I've learned not to jump to conclusions based upon what I see in a dream, especially when it concerns death. My sister (the one I saw in a casket) and I had a conversation about my dreams about people dying. She asked me how I respond when I have them.

I said, "Well, I don't want to call someone, especially if I don't know them personally, and just out of the clear blue say, 'I was just calling because I dreamed that you died.' I just wouldn't do that unless God dealt very strongly with me about that person or if I had this dream two or three times within a short time span and I knew without a doubt that God told me to deliver the message."

I am reluctant to deliver such messages; however, what I will do is first pray for that individual and their family because sometimes it may not be about the person seen in the dream. So normally, if God keeps showing me dreams about this person's death, I may call and have a caring conversation and let them know that I was thinking about them. I would be very prayerful when talking with them.

I've had this type of conversation with someone before when I dreamed that someone in their family died, not knowing that this particular family member was even sick. When I did call, I just asked how they were doing, and they said that person had been very sick. I told them I would be praying for them, and within weeks this person died. So God already knew that their loved one was going to die, and I believe that He wanted me to let them know that He was concerned about them during a time when they really needed comforting.

At My Friend's Deathbed

I once had a friend named Ms. Priscilla, whom I met at a church we both attended. Oh, Ms. Priscilla! To me she was the epitome of a young princess. She was in charge of the pastor's aides in the church, and she also was a great speaker. She had such a lovely smile as she spoke, and she always coordinated her outfits from head to toe. Every Sunday, I looked forward to seeing her beautiful smile as she encouraged us to worship the Lord. She was a cosmetologist, and I would often let her style my hair.

She was the only cosmetologist who finally talked me into getting my hair permed or relaxed. At that time, it was very thick and coarse, and I always had it straightened out with a hot comb. I knew that to straighten my hair was a long, hard, and tedious job, but I just didn't want any relaxer on it because I liked the way the thickness of my hair looked. I thought if I relaxed it, I would lose its coarseness. However, each time I went to her salon, she would say, "Marilyn, your hair is so coarse, you should let me give you a perm to relax and straighten it out." After many times of her "straightening out my hair," one day I finally gave in and told her to go ahead and put a perm in it—then I wondered what took me so long because I absolutely loved it. However, after many years of noticing that the relaxer seemed to make my hair thinner, I occasionally will wear my natural hair and press it (or straighten it) to give it a break from the perm, which I love also.

Ms. Priscilla was such a sweet woman. She wanted to have a baby but she was barren. Then one day she got pregnant, however, she had an affliction in her body and had to be very careful during her pregnancy. But God blessed her with the child she prayed for and gave her a beautiful little girl.

Later on in life her condition worsened, and I would sometimes take her to her doctor visits. As time went on I lost contact with her because I moved, and we no longer attended the same church. It was years later that one day I had a dream about Ms. Priscilla.

> I was sitting down by her bedside and she was very sick, in fact, she was dying and I said to her, "Ms. Priscilla, God told me to keep up with your daughter."

The next morning I was so burdened about what I had seen that I began to pray for her. I called my sister and told her what I saw in the dream and asked if she knew how I could contact Ms. Priscilla. She told me she would try to contact someone who might have her phone number. It was days later when my sister called me back and gave me the sad news—Ms. Priscilla had died. However, the good news was she didn't have to suffer anymore because she had gone home to be with the Lord.

I was so hurt and felt I had failed her and God by not staying in contact with her. I knew I was supposed to find her and let her know before she died what God had shown me. I repented for not trying hard enough to find her, and I learned a lesson from that experience, which is when God tells me to do something, I can't look to anyone else to do it for me because later after she had passed, I found the phone number. He told me I needed to do everything possible to perform the task He had given me and quickly.

I went to Ms. Priscilla's funeral, and I saw her daughter and spoke with her briefly. There were many people around her at the funeral, and it was not a good time for me to share with her what God had told me, but I was able to share it later.

There is a verse found in Psalm 116:15 about when a person dies and they have accepted Jesus Christ as their personal Savior, it says that their death is precious in the sight of God.

When our loved ones die, God is concerned about the living, and many times He is speaking something to us during these times. He is concerned about the people the dead are leaving behind, and I realized this when He spoke to me and said for me to keep up with her daughter. God already knew that I was not going to speak with Ms. Priscilla before she died, but I got the message that He spoke to me.

I will never know if there was something that Ms. Priscilla might have shared with me in her final days while she was on her deathbed. I would give anything now to have been there to listen to her last spoken words before she went to be with the Lord. But what I do feel good about is that God spoke to me as her life was slowly leaving her, and He told me to remember her daughter because apparently she was concerned about leaving her daughter behind.

This story is a reminder for us to be more attentive in sensitive situations and when we hear that voice say, "Go! It may be your last time to have that last conversation with them," we need to make haste and go.

Have you ever noticed that people who are getting ready to leave us sometimes have such spiritual insight in their last moments? It's as if they are seeing things or hearing a voice from heaven speak to them concerning things that are going to happen in the future; some have even experienced seeing their loved ones who previously went on to be with the Lord.

What I've discovered is, instead of being afraid of being around someone who is getting ready to leave us, we should want to be near them to hear what they have to share, their words of knowledge that we will never forget. Many times they will whisper comforting words for us to share with others whom they are leaving behind, to let them know not to worry about them because they are going to a better place, and to make sure our lives are in order and do whatever it takes spiritually to make sure they see us again.

7

Oh My Goodness, I'm Flying!

Flying to My Son's College

As a teenager I was always having dreams about flying. I really didn't think too much of it because that was during the time when the Jetsons were real popular. We saw flying cars and people; therefore, many times as a youngster, I just thought because I watched the *Jetsons*, maybe I wished I could fly too.

As years passed and I became an adult, I continued to have the flying dreams. One day when one of my sons went off to college, I was very concerned about him traveling in his car because he had been experiencing some major mechanical problems, and it was going to be a six-hour drive. However, he had to take that car—so we prayed together before he left. Later that afternoon, I fell asleep and had this dream:

I saw myself actually flying several feet up in the air (and it wasn't in a plane or helicopter) as I flew several feet above him all the way to the college campus. All I could see was the sky and sometimes a forest of trees. Then I saw him standing on the steps of a building on campus and he was smiling.

When I woke up, I was a little concerned because it had been over six hours and I had not heard from him, but on the other hand I felt that he was alright because of the dream I just had. When he did call, he apologized for taking so long to call, and as a mother, you know, I still had to give him a hard time for not calling me sooner. I then told him that I knew he had made it safely because God had revealed it to me in a dream.

God could have just had me wait until my son called to assure me that he had made it safely, but instead in the middle of the day, He let me go into a deep sleep to give me the comfort of knowing that my son had made it alright. I could have been a nervous wreck and not have been able to sleep or relax at all because this was his first trip away from home for such a lengthy time and he was in an unfamiliar place, but thank goodness I was able to get some rest.

God knew He needed to put me to sleep to keep me from pacing the floor and worrying about my son like I did when my other son went off to college. I did not rest at all as he took his trip off to college, which was many more miles away from home, and the way he had to travel to get there made me very nervous because he flew most of the way, then he had to ride the bus the remainder of his trip. So I guess God remembered what shape I was in when my other son left for college, and maybe He thought He'd better make me fall asleep so that He could show me that my son's travel was going to be safe and share with me the smile on my son's face.

God didn't verbally speak to me about my son's safe trip, but He communicated his safety to me in a method that I was quite familiar with (a dream), and He knew that I would understand that He was assuring me that my son was okay. Isn't it amazing how dreams can bring comfort to our concerns that we are faced with in everyday living? I prayed and asked God to guide my son there safely without any hurt, harm, danger, or mechanical problems, and God showed me that He answered my prayer through the dream. The other amazing thing about the dream was that I got to fly right along with him, even though he didn't see me. I know he felt the prayers that were being prayed, and he experienced the result of the prayers.

"I'm Lifting You Above Danger"

I still have dreams about flying occasionally. One day I heard a woman say that she had dreams about flying also and apparently many other people do too. I don't know what messages others receive as to the reason they are flying, but as I got older and started having these dreams again, God would speak to me in some of the dreams and say, "I'm lifting you up from your enemies." In most of the dreams I was always chased by someone, and then I would be lifted up in the air where they could not touch or harm me.

I recently had a dream about being in an earthquake:

There were several people about to get swallowed up in the earthquake, and in the dream I remembered how I would have dreams about when there was danger all around me God would lift me up into the air to safety. In the dream I started crying out to God to lift me up and let me fly from the danger of the earthquake, and I felt my body as it was being lifted up into midair and I was safe. The wonderful part about this dream was that as I was flying up in the air, God opened up the skies and took me right on into heaven. While I was there I saw many other people whose faces I knew. By the way, most of the people I saw actually are still living today.

When I woke up from this dream, I wondered if I had just dreamed about the Rapture. The end result of this dream is something that I live for and hope and pray for. After experiencing the many issues, struggles, and storms of life, and the dangers that are surrounding me in this world, my hope is that one day I will be caught up in the air and taken to that heavenly place to live forever. I am still praying about this dream, especially the earthquake, because of where it took place. One thing I do know is that if God allows for an earthquake to hit close to home, I definitely want to be in a position spiritually for God to hear me when I cry out to Him for help. I want Him to come to my rescue, whether He saves me from the earthquake down here on earth and I live through it, or He just takes me on to that heavenly place. Another thing I know is that I will be safe in His arms as long as I have a relationship with Him.

The Translation

I once had a dream about being translated to another city in the spiritual realm. One of the *Merriam-Webster's Collegiate Dictionary* definitions of *translation* is "an act, process, or instance of translating." One of the definitions of *translating* is "to bear, remove, or change from one place, state, form, or appearance to another, and to convey (which can mean "to carry away secretly or to cause to pass from one place to another" to heaven or to a non-temporal condition without death."

> The Spirit of the Lord was carrying me warp-speed up into the sky until I began to get very, very cold. Then I felt ice touch my body, and at that point I became frightened. The Spirit of God spoke to me and said, "Are you afraid?" and I answered "Yes." So He released my body from the point wherever I was and within a blink of an eye I was in another state on the ground. I knew I was not at home because I landed in front of a business and saw a sign on the door with an out-of-state phone number on it.

When I woke up I hurried to look up the area code to find out where in the world God had translated me because it was not an area code that looked familiar. God did not give me the interpretation of the dream at that time, but later I believed I knew what it was all about because the area code was a phone number in Alabama. I had been translated to Alabama, and it was a beautiful, clear, and sunny day. This was approximately a year before God told me and Nate that it was time for him to get his first book published. Well, after Nate worked on his book project, God blessed him with a contract with a publishing company located in Alabama, and they have published his first two books. I believe that is what God revealed to me.

Speaking of translations, there are a few Bible stories of men who were actually translated from one place to another. Enoch did not see death because God actually just took him on into heaven without him dying; this episode is found in Genesis 5:24. Elijah was just carried away in a chariot by a whirlwind right on into heaven, again taken into heaven without dying, found in 2 Kings 2:1–12, and God translated Philip to another city after he baptized a man, found in Acts 8:35–40. Wow!

I know the translation happened to me in a dream, but I believe it can happen in real life, as it did in Bible days. Wow, that would be great if God decides to take me in that manner! I hope He has someone there to witness it, just as He allowed Elisha to witness Elijah's translation, I wouldn't want anyone to be worried about me. Plus it would be such an awesome act of God, a powerful and miraculous event for someone to witness and then be able to share their testimony with others in this present time. It could happen!

We don't always understand the reason we have these adventurous dreams, such as seeing ourselves flying. I believe there is a meaning to be explored. Why do I believe this? Because He has helped me to understand these dreams as I see myself flying. For the longest time, I was not really trying to get an understanding, but after having these dreams for so many years, I began to ask. Have you asked Him about your dreams lately? I encourage you to do so.

8

A Child's Encounter

Nate shared some events with me that took place at an early age in his life, which involved having encounters with the Spirit of God. One particular event began to unfold as early as when he was in kindergarten. His kindergarten teacher was a person who demanded the very best from all of her students. Her name was Mrs. Crouch, though many of her students thought her name should have been Mrs. Grouch! To those like Nate, she used a scare tactic that involved make-believe hungry monsters that would gouge out and eat the eyes of those children who were not so intimidated by her threats of punishment. During one of his many rebellious episodes, Nate called her bluff and she opened the door to the low-ceilinged attic, picked him up, and put his head into the opening.

She yelled, "Nate, if you don't say you're sorry for what you did, the eye-eating monster is going to get you!"

He remembered not being intimidated by what the monster would do to him, but he was more interested in what it would look like. What he saw at that time didn't seem to be so fierce or monstrous, but he saw a set of eyes that just stared at him.

Then he heard a voice that said, "Don't be afraid. I won't hurt you."

Nate replied, "I'm not scared."

Mrs. Crouch obviously didn't hear what he heard or see what he saw because she pulled him down and asked, "What did you see up there?"

"I saw some eyes, and they told me not to be scared . . ."

She simply replied, "I knew it!"

Years later when Nate became an adult, he was reminded of that moment after he had acknowledged and accepted his call to the ministry at thirty-one years of age. Mrs. Crouch showed up at their church on the very same day the pastor accepted the fact and called Nate to join the rest of the ministers on the pulpit roster.

Mrs. Crouch, who belonged to the neighborhood church down the street, was sitting on the first row at their church. After Nate got up from his seat and joined the pastor on the pulpit, Mrs. Crouch leaped from her seat at about eighty-something years old. She began to scream out statements such as, "I told you! God showed me when he was my student that he was one of His. I also told you God said to stay out of His business because it was going to be so!" Then she began to dance in the Spirit!

This caught everyone by surprise except the pastor and the deacon board. After services Nate asked, "Pastor, what in the world was Mrs. Crouch talking about?"

"She was talking about you, man. Yesterday I was asked to meet with the deacon board at one of the deacon's homes to discuss stopping you from preaching and also to stop your ordination." Nate said this was probably due to the fact that he had less than perfect teenage years, though he was always a church member.

The pastor went on to say, "During this meeting, Mrs. Crouch barged her way into the meeting room and began telling us to stop the meeting."

She said, "I was cleaning my house and God spoke to me about what was taking place here. He told me to come over here and warn all you men to get out of His business. Nathan is one of His elected sons, and no man can stop what He has planned for his life!"

This reminds me of when God revealed a vision to Ezekiel and lifted him up in the Spirit and took him to a gate of the Lord's house. There he saw men who were devising mischief and giving wicked counsel in that city. The Spirit of the Lord fell upon Ezekiel and told him to prophesy to them and tell them that He knew the things that came into their minds, every one of them (Ezekiel 11:1–5). God has a way of reminding us that He is everywhere at all times and He knows about every plot that others are planning against us.

Over the Years

In the duration of years between Nate being in kindergarten and accepting his call to the ministry at age thirty-one, he remembered hearing conversations between some of his cousins and aunts from his mother's family concerning a minister whom God was going to raise up in the family. These aunts and cousins were mostly members of another neighborhood church and stated on several occasions that they had dreams of a man called to the ministry who would come through their family and would have a great impact on the Kingdom of God and the entire world.

His grandmother on his dad's side would often tell them similar stories, and two of the men on that side of the family later went into the Gospel ministry for a few years and then stopped preaching. One day he heard his grandmother ask both of them, "Did God call you? If not, don't play with Him! God did not show me either of you, but y'all will soon know who God had revealed to me."

Nate often wondered who this preacher would be like, considering some of the prophets of Bible times. You see, as a child he often would imagine himself to be one of the great prophets he had learned about in Sunday school and Bible training classes. He thought about how neat it would be to do some of the miracles they performed.

Nate began to feel God's Spirit tug at his soul, sometimes showing him things in dreams and other times he would hear voices speaking. We know this is no mystery because Samuel, the prophet, heard voices from God when he was called and Paul as well heard a voice from the Lord when he was called. There were times when Nate's grandmother would sit him down and say to him, "God loves you so much, Nathan, and He wants to use and bless you."

She later told him, "Nathan, you are a chosen son of God and you are going to preach God's Word." This is something that went right over his head, and neither did he believe her.

For some strange reason, Nate's mother was not comfortable letting him go to parties as a teenager or just hang out with the other boys or girls. Once when he was fourteen years of age, he wanted to go to a party down the street from their house, but she would not consent for him to go, alleging that he had to go to Sunday school the next morning. Stubbornly,

Nate strongly accused her of being unfair and when she left home, he went to the party anyway. While there, he was stabbed in the left side of his chest and almost bled to death before making it to the hospital. By the time the ambulance got him to the hospital, the doctor told his dad that if the blade would have been a bullet, it would have ruptured a vein and he would have died of a heart attack. His mother told him that it was because he disobeyed her, but he also knew it was a much deeper issue. From that point, his eyes were opened and he said he never again argued with his parents or did he ever again complain about going to church or Sunday school.

There was always something about Bible stories that intrigued him, and he fell in love with the Bible characters early in life because of the things they did. For most of his youthful life he had rejected the idea that he was to become a preacher. It was the furthest thing from his mind, no matter what people said to him or what they said God had shown them concerning him. However, eventually Nate accepted his calling into the ministry.

So now not only can small children have dreams, but they too can see visions. There may be others who were of a young age and had no idea what was going on who may have experienced something similar; however, as they grew older, God put them in the company of someone who could help them understand what was going on and know that it was God all along making contact with them.

Many people have seen these special callings in children or that there was something special about certain children as they were growing up. It is so important for us as adults who have more experience and are seasoned in our gifts that when we discern such gifts in small children, we pray for them so they won't be misled and get involved in the wrong spirits of this world.

It was good that Nate was raised up in church and received the spiritual teaching. By reading the stories in the Bible of how God communicated with different individuals, sometimes through dreams and visions, he would soon understand that it was God speaking to him.

God used Nate's kindergarten teacher, Mrs. Crouch, to discern that her little student had a special calling on his life. All those years, it is obvious that she had been praying for him, and he didn't even know it until the time came when she found out that he had accepted his call into the ministry.

Here we see that God communicated to Mrs. Crouch that she had a student whom she was to keep in her prayers and he was going to grow up to be a preacher. When the time came many years later, God spoke to her to go and tell the pastor, deacons, and others who were having a private meeting to stay out of His business because He had called Nate to the ministry and then God blessed her to live long enough to see it come to pass.

Nate talks about how he was glad that Mrs. Crouch listened to God and took notice of him while he was her little student and prayed for him. Here we have Mrs. Crouch, who paid attention to God when He told her that there was something taking place in a private meeting and that He wanted her to go and give them a message from Him. She believed God and responded to Him by not being afraid to confront the church leaders.

Nate is thankful to God that his mother saw to it that he stayed in church and thankful that Mrs. Crouch let God use her to pray for him and confirm his calling. He's thankful his grandmother prayed for him and told him, before God took her home, that God had called him to preach, and so thankful and grateful that God spared his life many times, and that God gave him many chances to finally say yes to Him. As an adult, God still shows up with the eyes peeking out of the vast darkness to remind Nate that it was Him who was there calling and drawing him near to Him when he was of an early age.

God has ways of communicating with young children or performing miraculous tasks before their eyes, so when they get old enough they will know it was Him with them all along. I am reminded about the story of King David when he was just a youth (see 1 Samuel 17). He told Saul that he knew it was the Lord who was with him when he killed a lion and a bear at that young age because it certainly was not of his natural strength. We should listen to our children when they come to us and say they had a dream. Ask them questions: What images did they see? What was said in the dream? As a parent we need to know. Whatever they saw or heard while they were sleeping, we can address it by either praying with them or just knowing that you may need to monitor what they're watching or the video games they're playing.

By taking the time to ask our children questions when they're having dreams, it shows that we are concerned about what they are seeing while they're sleeping. We may even discover that God is dealing with them at an early age. We must ask God to teach us how to mentor our children or see to it that they are mentored in the gifts He's given them. This is important because sometimes as parents we don't always pay that close attention to what our children are experiencing when it comes to dreams. These dreams may reveal signs that they may have special gifts, but if we don't' realize it, as they grow up there will be many distractions that can carry them away from their true purpose and destiny.

Therefore, as parents we have to be aware of what's going on with our children. Have you ever asked God what your child's purpose in life is? When we ask about their purpose while they are still babies, we can guide them in the right direction as we let God lead us. Remember to train up a child in the way of the Lord because as they get older and at some point reach those crossroads in life, and it's for certain that they will, they can recall those godly teachings that were instilled in them when they were young and then make the right decisions.

9

Why Say Grace?

I was at a supermarket and went to the counter for a certain product and noticed the counters were empty in that section. As I was checking out, I asked the cashier why the counters were empty, and she said, "Those products had to be taken off the shelf because of possible contamination."

I had this dream many years before there were so many reports of recalls for this particular product and many others. After having that dream, I wondered if I should share the dream with Nate because this was one of his favorite foods, but I could just hear him saying, "Now, we just have to pray over it because I'm not giving it up."

So I prayed about it and didn't tell him right away. However, it bothered me so much that one day I decided to share the dream with him. I thought that if he ever ate some of this particular product and it made him sick, I didn't know if I could forgive myself for not sharing the dream with him. So I shared the dream and suggested that maybe we should just stop buying it all altogether. To my surprise, he asked me, "Well, do *you* think we should stop eating it?" I was surprised at his response because I had thought he would reject the very thought of giving it up.

So I paused a moment and asked, "Well, what do you think?" He threw the question back at me again. I guess he was saying, "Well, you said the Lord showed you something about it, what do you think we should do?" I said, "Well, why don't we pray about it to get a full understanding of what God is saying?" So we prayed about it and believed that God was telling us to be prayerful about not only what we ate, but what we purchased. So we accepted that God was telling us to be conscientious of this, and we made the decision to continue to buy the product. That was over ten years ago.

As usual, time goes on, and we forget about some of the dreams we have. If there is nothing in the media or if it's not a hot topic, it isn't usually discussed. I'm not so quick to say a dream is from God unless God gives me the interpretation right then or if later that dream comes true. I had this dream long before there was so much cautiousness to be taken because of contaminated products at the level it has been.

Then, one day the fearful event happened in 2008. We received a letter stating a product that we had purchased had been recalled and to take it back to the store. This happened to be the very same type of product I had dreamed about several years ago. Well, the letter came a little too late. We had already eaten it, but thank God we didn't get sick. We always say grace before we eat or drink anything. Why? First, to thank God for giving us our daily bread, and then we ask Him to purify it, to bless it, to let it be nourishment to our bodies, and to not let it harm us.

In the letter, there was a phone number to call, so I decided to call them. When I spoke with one of their associates, I told her we had received a letter to return the purchased item back to the store because it had been recalled due to possible contamination; however we had already eaten it. She asked if we had gotten sick from eating it. I replied, "I can't recall us feeling ill around the time we ate it." So after answering all the questions she asked, we both resolved that it appeared that we were not affected by the product, and we ended the call.

That situation reminded me to always pray even when I go grocery shopping or eat out. This same kind of product that I had purchased and was warned to return to the store was the same type of product that I had dreamed about several years before. Was God, way back then, sending me a warning to be prayerful of what I buy or to be prayerful of what I put in my body? The Word of God tells us to acknowledge Him in all ours ways and He will direct our paths. I believe that applies even to where to shop and what to purchase.

In all thy ways acknowledge him, and he shall direct thy paths (Proverbs 3:6).

I believe that regardless of whatever we take into our bodies, we should always say grace and ask God to bless it and not let it harm us. This is not meant to be a discussion of what to eat. Since the Bible days, there have been many health issues with a lot of products we put in our bodies. Some are not even mentioned in the Bible because they have been man-made; however, I can say the message was to be aware, be careful, and pray over everything. Jesus told the disciples that everyone who believes in Him and is baptized shall be saved (born again), and if they drink any deadly thing unintentionally, it shall not hurt them.

They shall take up serpents; and if they drink any deadly thing, it shall not hurt them; they shall lay hands on the sick, and they shall recover (Mark 16:18).

I pray for all industries that make products that are being provided to consumers, whether to consume or to put on our bodies, for the health, safety, and welfare of the people. I thank God for those in charge of inspecting all products that they will continue to find the hazardous problems and contaminated products before they are sold to consumers.

We must pray and ask God to help us obey His laws and keep His ordinances so He can bless our land and everything that it yields.

And I will rebuke the devourer for your sakes, and he shall not destroy the fruits of your ground; neither shall your vine cast her fruit before the time in the field, saith the Lord of hosts. And all nations shall call you blessed: for ye shall be a delightsome land, saith the Lord of hosts (Malachi 3:11–12).

Here God was informing me by way of a dream about being careful of what we purchased at the supermarket. This was a message to me that when God shows me warnings to protect the safety and welfare of people that I should share those warnings because I could possibly prevent them from encountering serious health issues. God gave us certain herbs for medicine and vegetables and certain meats for food, and

He is concerned about what we let enter into our bodies. He will warn us if we're about to put something in our bodies that could be harmful; however, it's a good thing to always say grace first.

This raised awareness for me to not be so careless or nonchalant about what I put in the body that God gave me. Actually our bodies really belong to Him, which means we should be prayerful in all things. God is concerned about every aspect of our lives, and He lets us know that by looking out for us even when we don't know or realize that we really need to be aware of certain things.

Nate and I decided to continue to purchase the product after I had the dream; however, as always, we gave grace and asked God to not let it bring harm to us. So years later when we did consume this product that posed a threat to our health because of possible contamination, God protected us from getting sick and even from getting sick unto death.

We shouldn't limit saying grace to only what we eat and drink. I was taught to say grace concerning everything. Therefore, I pray before I take any prescription drugs or supplements. It doesn't matter what it is, I have learned to pray about whatever is going into this body and also what I'm putting on my body.

Do you ever pray about the over-the-counter medication you are about to give your children? Think about it: sometimes your child may be allergic to something and you don't know it, and they could have allergic reactions that could make them very sick. These are things most of us don't think about until we hear that some child became ill. There are many dangerous side effects that come from taking medications—the labels warn us of such—so I make it a point to always pray before I take them. Yes, I thank Him for the medications just as I thank Him for the food and drink. After all, medication has saved and prolonged many lives.

Why do we say grace? Because we are thankful for our daily bread and we believe God will keep anything deadly from harming us, if we unknowingly put contaminated products in our bodies. We can never pray too much, especially when it concerns our health. There are always alerts going out warning consumers about products being recalled because of possible contamination. When we are informed about products that we are about to consume that could possibly be contaminated, it pays to listen, pay attention, and take heed. If we somehow just didn't get the warning message and we consume whatever the product was, just keep in mind that we always should say grace before we consume anything.

10

Keeping Our School Campuses Safe

There have been several shootings at school and college campuses in the twenty-first century like I've never seen before in my lifetime, which is quite disturbing and very frightening, especially for the people who are on campus. Months before one of the most notorious school shootings happened at the end of the twentieth century, I had the following dream.

> There were a group of students on a panel at their school discussing what could possibly be done to stop the shootings on school campuses, and I saw a gun in the midst of them.

I woke up wondering why I would have such a dream, so I called someone whom I could share the dream with and we prayed about it to get an understanding. Then, months later, this horrifying shooting happened. The people were so terrified and scared, as well as wondering what could have happened or caused such a thing to happen at their school. I knew then that it was God who had showed me this dream.

He was telling me that it was very important that I pray for school campuses and to tell others to pray. He knew that things were getting ready to take a turn for the worse at not just one campus but several.

It just so happened that one of the people I shared the dream with was acquainted with a lady who was also very disturbed about what happened, and she shared with me that this lady was organizing a prayer march to be held at a school campus. The purpose of the prayer march was to pray for God's protection over this campus and campuses all over the world and to bring comfort and healing to those affected by and surrounding that incident.

I immediately wanted to know more about the prayer march, so she suggested that I contact the organizer of the march. I made the call to this lady, shared my dream with her, and told her I wanted to join in the prayer march. Many people gathered on the campus and we prayed as we walked the grounds of the campus, then we went into the school chapel to pray for the safety of campuses all around the world. As of this date I have not heard of any shootings or lockdowns at this particular school.

Many parents have had to receive disappointing messages that their children, who went to school to get an education, where they thought could be one of the safest places for them to be, were barricaded or in a lockdown. These students were not at the wrong place at the wrong time, but they were at the right place doing the right thing—getting an education.

We may not always hear our children talking about their concerns for safety at their school; however, each time they hear about these incidents or even experience one, their families become fearful all over again. Our children need to be able to go to school or college to focus on their education, and the parents need to be able to believe that when their children are on campus they are safe.

When these incidents happen, at that very moment it takes the focus off the reason the staff and students are there, families' lives are turned upside down, and some families are never the same afterwards. Everyone is paranoid, not knowing if and when there will be a copycat incident. But the students, parents, staff, people in the communities, and others who are affected by these tragedies are courageous and brave enough to keep going and not let the tragedies overcome them to the point where they just give up; I believe it's done with much prayer.

On the other hand, what should and can be done to make us feel safer and have some sense of security? I truly believe in the power of prayer and that God is able to keep our campuses safe; however, we must continue to pray for the best security measures to be taken to help keep these incidents from taking place. I am encouraged to know there are campuses still having prayer; however, there are still some schools that prohibit students from praying. But let a shooting occur at that school, then all of a sudden everybody wants to come together and pray because that's the right thing to do. I remember when I was in school, we always went to the auditorium to have devotions and we prayed. When my children were very young and in school, I would not have them wait until they got to school to pray, but we would have prayer together before leaving home.

When we don't keep godly values in our land, it is too easy to start accepting other values that are not of God. If we don't seek God for the best solutions, we may end up resorting to ways that may not help resolve our problems but make them worse. We know this is a country of free speech and freedom of religion, however God commands that we keep His commandments and obey His laws. When we don't include God's commandments in our man-made laws, we begin to disregard His laws for our land and that could mean much trouble in the land.

Right now, education is a hot topic and it's so important to be educated, from the child learning centers to the adult educational institutions. People want to know that they have some sense of security while they are trying to get an education and to know that their children are safe while at school. Seeking God for solutions to the shooting crises is the most effective way to approach this issue, but we have to be willing to want to hear from Him and follow His instructions.

I am not saying that when we pray that we will not get caught up in tragedies, or that because we pray we will be saved from being a victim since that isn't always true. There have been many innocent people whose lives were taken who prayed when they knew they were going to be a victim, and only God knows the answer as to the reason their lives were taken or why someone was fatally wounded.

But what I am saying is that it shouldn't stop us from praying and seeking God for solutions to these matters. He can stop it from becoming worse. He can show someone the signs of what could be about to take place in enough time so that some kind of action can be taken to prevent any tragedy.

I encourage everyone to continue in prayer every day for the safety of our campuses and to pray with their children before they go to school. Those having discussions concerning how to make the schools safer, I encourage you to seek God for the best solutions in preventing these tragedies because many innocent children and adults did not deserve to leave us so soon in such a horrific way.

I also encourage the young people who are participating in devotions to continue to stay involved in prayer and encourage other students to be excited about going to school to get their education. Who knows, the effects of these young people prayers just may save a life.

11

The Great Recession

I saw many people in line at a bank, and as I looked, I could see that the line started inside the bank and extended outside onto a walkway. The people were not able get access to their money through the ATM machines, and the bank would only allow them to have a certain amount of their own money.

I had this dream in March of 2006. I remember it vividly because that same day, I was so disturbed because of what I saw that I called my mother and asked her if she remembered anything concerning the Great Depression. She began to tell me things her father shared with her. She said she remembered some of the things they had to go through during the latter part of the Great Depression. She shared how my grandfather said there was very little and times were extremely hard, but God helped them through those tough times.

Just think about it for a minute: not only was it a Great Depression, but there were no vaccines for certain diseases;

therefore, many people in those times became very ill and died. I can't imagine how horrible the times were, not only worrying about whether your family would have enough to survive on, but also having to deal with the incurable illnesses all at the same time.

I know there are people in situations even now who are probably still feeling the effects of the recession—lost jobs, homes, businesses, no health care, millions of dollars lost— and it seems as though there's nowhere to go or no one to turn to for help. I encourage you to keep believing and trusting in God because He hasn't forgotten you. I remember discussing this dream with Nate, and we decided we had better focus on getting out of debt because if that dream came true, things were going to get really tough in our economy. I shared the dream with a few close friends and prayer partners and asked them to pray and focus on getting out of debt and ask God to take care of their families during some possible difficult times ahead.

Sometimes a dream like this one is not easy to share with others. As optimistic as I am, people have a tendency to think that I favor delivering news of doom and gloom or being the bearer of bad news, when that's the furthest thing from the truth. God has always warned His people so He can prepare them, whether it's about a great blessing or a catastrophic event that's about to take place. My spiritual mother used to tell me, "Marilyn, to be forewarned is to be forearmed." Therefore, God will warn and prepare us for things that are to come upon us before they happen, and He may provide us with a way of escape.

One might ask if God has ever shown me that our economy is going to get better and when. Has God ever showed me a new home for someone, or a husband or wife? You may ask if I saw someone driving a brand-new car or if their child is getting a full scholarship into college. Not to say there is anything wrong with desiring to have these things, because He did say for us to seek first His Kingdom and righteousness and He will give us things according to His will. He also said that if we delight ourselves in Him, He will give us the desires of our heart.

I believe God has shown people their home before they moved in; their spouse, as in my case; or even a vehicle. He showed me in a dream that He was going to bless Nate and me with a particular vehicle, which soon afterward we received. Therefore, God does desire to bless us with our daily needs, and He will also bless us with the desires of our hearts. He will sometimes let us get a glimpse of how He is going to bless us.

God reveals many things to certain people; it just seems as if I mostly get messages of warnings. Who wouldn't want a warning that something bad may be going to happen to them before it happens and the knowledge that God may be warning them so it can be avoided? I would certainly want to know. By the same token, who wouldn't want to be encouraged that God had a wonderful blessing coming their way? I know I would.

It has been several years since I had that particular dream. Many people have had many misfortunes due to this recession. I am told that this has been one of the worst economic times we have had in America since the Great Depression, and from what I have heard, we may have been on the verge of another one. This has not only affected America, but this recession has had a great impact on many countries around the world. Some countries were affected worse than others.

God wants us to depend on Him as our source because He has many resources. We have to keep the faith because He is our ultimate provider. Jesus taught us not to worry about life's necessities in Matthew 6:30–34 when He reminded us that our heavenly Father knows our needs. Sometimes when my faith gets a little shaky, I will read the entire chapter of Hebrews 11, which always encourages and helps me to keep having faith and trusting in God no matter what it looks like and no matter the outcome.

Sometimes we don't want to accept the truth. We would rather someone come to us and say things like, there will never be another great recession or depression ever again, or that we will not be affected by whatever happens. However, that would not be realistic because famines, recessions, and depressions affect everybody in some kind of way. There have been a lot of churchgoers and non-churchgoers alike who have been affected by this Great Recession.

Just because we have to go through some tough times doesn't mean that God doesn't still love us. He wants us to cast all our cares upon Him because He does care for us. When we trust God with all of our heart, soul, and mind, it doesn't mean that we still will not have to go through tough times and have to do without some of the things we are used to having. It doesn't mean that sometimes things still won't go all bad; it doesn't mean that trouble won't come our way. Just remember He will keep us in perfect peace if we keep our mind stayed on Him, even through tough times.

There comes a time when we have to be content with whatever we have and whatever we have to do without and learn to still trust God in whatever state He has us in, knowing that He will supply all of our needs according to His riches in glory by Christ Jesus, even as Paul told us in Philippians 4:11 and 19.

God knows what the future holds for all of us, and He desires for those of us who trust in Him to have peace. He sees all the suffering that we encounter, but if we continue to trust in Him and live for Him, He has rewards for every one of us. He will lead us to the Promised Land to live with Him forever in our very own mansion that He has prepared just for us in the new city. We are not here to stay forever; there is a brighter day and a better place in the new city where we will live with God for eternity. I encourage you to seek Him daily and look forward to living in that new city.

Many people say the economy will get better. Truthfully, I don't know, because God hasn't spoken that to me nor has He shown me anything other than what I shared with you about the people I saw standing in line at a bank. I know in some parts of the world this happened during the recession. But that doesn't mean that He hasn't shown someone else that it will get better and even when it will get better. He just showed me years before it happened that the economy was going to be going through some struggling times. Even the Great Depression didn't last forever; it took some years for the economy to get back to a normal recovery, but eventually the economy blossomed. Therefore, I believe we can also have a recovery from this Great Recession, but I don't know when or how it will happen, nor if God will allow us to have a full recovery.

God can help our economy. There have been many times when He sent messages through His prophets to be delivered to kings that if the king and the people of that land would repent and obey His laws, He would overturn situations that had come upon their land. There were times when the kings listened and obeyed the word from the Lord, and God did not allow that nation to have to endure hard times. But we have to do it God's way. This is not like Burger King, where you can "have it your way." We can't do it our way in God's Kingdom!

But as I read my Bible, I know that there will be a generation that is going to be faced with even more devastating and troubling times than we are facing now. There will be a time of great tribulation—those times are coming. Whether we will live to see those times or not, there will be other generations in our families that will.

If we believe there will be trying times that our future generations will have to face, God holds us accountable to teach and prepare them with the Word of God. Shame on us if after we have died and those troublesome times come, that a generation asks, "Why didn't anyone tell us what was to come or tell us some of the things that we were going to have to encounter? Why didn't anyone prepare us the best they knew how? Why didn't they teach us to pray and encourage us to keep faith in God during these troubled times?"

God has always instructed the older generation to teach the younger generation and commanded us to teach our children the ways of the Lord. We are to teach them how to pray, believe God's Word, and have faith that no matter how tough society becomes, they can be strong and trust in the Lord.

There may be someone who is going through some very difficult times right now. In the 17th chapter of 1 Kings there was a prophet named Elijah who prophesied to Ahab that there was going to be a famine in the land and there would be no rain for years. God also spoke to Elijah and told him to go and hide himself by a brook, and there he would drink out of that brook. God also told him that He had commanded the ravens to feed him there at the brook. The Bible says that Elijah obeyed God and drank out of the brook, and the ravens brought him some bread and meat.

After awhile since there was no rain, the brook dried up and God told Elijah to go to a widow woman's house because He had commanded the widow woman to sustain him. When he arrived, she told him that she only had a handful of meal in a barrel and a little oil in a pot. She was planning to cook their last meal, eat it, and prepare to die. But the man of God told her to make him a little cake first and afterward to make some for her and her son.

He told her that God said that the barrel of meal would not waste, neither would the container of oil fail, until the day that the Lord sent rain upon the earth. She did what the prophet said and she, Elijah, and her household ate for many days. So the barrel of meal never went empty, and neither did she run out of oil, which was the word of the Lord spoken through Elijah, the prophet. God does perform miracles for us during hard times.

This story reminds me of a woman who ran out of food. She and her family didn't have anything to eat, and surprisingly someone showed up with bags of groceries at her front door and told her that the Lord had told them to go shopping for her. I have heard similar stories. So there are times when God will touch a person's heart to just show up on someone's doorstep and surprise them with exactly what they needed. The person in need may not have communicated it to anyone but God, but He heard them and then touched someone's heart to provide them with whatever they needed so they would know that their prayers were heard.

Are you a modern-day Elijah? Has God spoken to you and asked you to go and bless a family who is hungry or is in need during this recession? Have you had a widow woman's experience during the time of the Great Recession? Has God ever spoken to you to be a blessing to someone and you obeyed Him, knowing you barely had enough for your own family to live on, but then God blessed you with more than you had before you blessed them?

As trying times will come, our next generation of families must be able to keep faith in God and keep trusting Him, no matter how they see the waves of ups and downs in the economy, no matter who they see fall from the faith, because God never changes. He is always with us through the hard and tough times no matter what it looks like, just as He is with us during the good times.

If we listen more to God during difficult times and pay more attention to Him, we just might realize that God wants to get involved in our situations. We might discover that He has ways of providing for us that we may never have considered.

12

9/11

Since America experienced the terrible tragedy of 9/11, it's been a very controversial topic as to why it happened and who was really behind it. I don't know all the details of what was behind 9/11 nor who was involved in what brought this terrible tragedy to our homeland. However, what I do know is that there are people to whom God had communicated, one way or another, that something catastrophic was coming upon America's soil. He had revealed it to Nate and me in a dream and a vision.

One particular night, approximately one month prior to the attack on America, Nate sat in his recliner, hoping that it would, as it had always done, put him to sleep. However, this night he remained wide awake. The hour approached almost 2:00 a.m. Knowing that he had to get up at 4:30 a.m. to go to work, Nate got into bed and hoped for the best. At approximately 2:35 a.m. he felt himself drifting off into what he thought was a well-anticipated sleep, but he began slipping into a trancelike state that he could not snap out of no matter how he fought it. What I'm about to share is an experience that Nate encountered about 9/11.

It felt like a severe blood rush to his head, and as it settled, he saw himself standing in the middle of a street in the midst of a gray hazy dawn. Looking to his right, he saw an enormous building, resembling an office-type building, with several floors and windows, and it appeared that there was a tall steeple tower at the top. He quickly looked to the left and saw an identical building; the building's top was obscured by a cloud. The buildings were not only enormous in size, but they reached far into the sky.

He thought to himself that he had never seen any buildings or structures that tall in his whole life. He wondered, What in the world am I seeing, and where am I?

Suddenly, in the clouds that covered the top of the building to his left, he could hear what he thought to be thunder, and he saw flashes of bright light. He thought that a storm was brewing. The clouds were dark and began to turn and move about frantically.

He noticed that the clouds were forming figures, which began to walk toward the building on his right side, each making noises that seem to express extreme anger or agitation. The first figure was that of a giant fierce lion, which moved with a flying type of speed to the building to his right, and as it flew on top of the building, it dropped something on it and quickly moved to the building on the left and did the same, then disappeared into the clouds. One after the other several beasts formed from the clouds and followed the lion, doing the same things and disappearing into the clouds. There were seven beasts in total.

When he looked back to the building on the right, all he saw was what looked like a pile of smoking dung. Amazed, he quickly looked to his left and saw that building beginning to crumble from the clouds toward the ground. He began to run down the street, terrified, not knowing what was happening, and suddenly the vision ended.

After Nate had that vision, he began to ask, "Lord, what did I just see?" Then immediately Nate began to see another vision.

He saw the black sky with a few scattered stars, then as many times before, when the Lord would reveal His presence to him, a huge face appeared. First closed eyes would open to a piercing look at him, bright white with dark pupils. Only this time there was something very different in the eyes. They were grayish, not white, and the pupils were not dark, but red with live dancing flames.

The nose appeared to be broader than usual with the U-shaped split (instead of open nostrils as before), with a few long straight whiskers on both sides, and a snarling expression. The mouth appeared half-open with spaced round teeth. As it opened wide, huge canines appeared as fangs, drooling with saliva and blood, like a fierce beast after a kill. He then realized that it was not that wonderfully pleasant face he always saw, but the face of an angry lion, very agitated about something.

As the vision disappeared, he was totally terrified, wondering what he could have done to make the Lord so angry with him. He immediately went straightaway into the living room. He knelt down to pray, repenting, inquiring, and begging for insight. For days afterward, the Lord began to speak to Nate concerning the gross hypocrisies in this country. *Repent* was God's warning!

We didn't understand the vision that Nate saw about running down the streets of Manhattan, NY, and the various beasts flying over two buildings until the day of 9/11. Neither of us had ever been to Manhattan, New York, nor did the World Trade Center Towers ever come to our minds, so we went into prayer for the interpretation.

Approximately one month later, I happened to be home the morning of 9/11 when my sister called me and said to turn the television on to the news channel because something terrible was happening. As my eyes were glued to the television for several hours, watching this terrible tragedy, I saw one building fall and the dust from the building filled the streets and covered people as they frantically were running for their lives. That's when I saw the scenario of a dream flash right before my eyes that I had in 1995. I panicked and said, "This is what I saw in a dream."

> I saw people running in a downtown area away from a cloud of dust in a street, some holding briefcases in their hands. They were frantically running from the cloud of dust coming down into the streets. The people were so terrified and crying out for help.

At this point I called my sister back and told her this was what I saw in the dream back in 1995, and then I grabbed my dream diary to see if I had written it down, and there it was written just as I had seen it.

I remember the day of 9/11 so vividly because when I talked with my husband, who was at work, we both said, that this was what God had shown us approximately one month prior and six years prior. We were both so distraught, wondering why we didn't know the interpretation of what we had seen in the dream and vision so that we could have warned someone before it happened. I just remembered that I had only shared my dream with him and my sister, who suggested that I start recording my dreams, and he had shared the visions he had with me and some guys at work.

On the day of 9/11, this bothered my husband so much that he sent e-mails to leaders to share what God had shown us. As we look back, we wonder if we would have researched and thought more about the tall buildings that appeared to have a steeple tower on it, and then figured out since the buildings were so tall it was not a steeple tower but an antenna. Then maybe, the World Trade Center would have come to mind, since they were two enormously tall buildings. Until this date, we wish we could have known more so that we could have warned someone and possibly lives would have been saved.

This still lives with us, as it does so many people, and especially the loved ones and friends of those whose lives were lost. God knew before 9/11 happened that it was going to happen. Many have asked, "How could God allow this to happen?" We don't always have the answers to such tragedies. We don't know the reason God did not give us the interpretation of what He showed us so we could have warned someone. We were told later that other people had dreams of 9/11 also before it happened, and I don't know if God told them exactly what they saw when they had the dream, or if they shared it with others before 9/11.

Every year on 9/11 when memorial services are held, it is a very emotional time for America. Our hearts are so heavy because we are reliving the moments again. Nate and I also get emotional during these times because in the spiritual dimension we saw this tragedy unfold before it happened, but we didn't know to send out a warning. We questioned God, "Why didn't we know the meaning of the dream and vision? Why didn't we know the date of when it was going to happen? Would anyone have listened to us if we had sent warnings out? Would those who could have taken action to prevent something from happening even taken us seriously or would they have laughed at us, mocked us, and said we were crazy?"

For days, weeks, and months after 9/11, I saw a nation of people put aside all their differences, their prejudices, and their own agendas, and put their hearts into reaching out to help the hurting and the harmed. There were those who were affected in one way or another, reaching out to people who were injured and to families and friends of the loved ones who died in this tragedy. There were people giving of their time and money toward the cause. I saw signs of unity; signs of "United We Stand" were all over America. I saw so much love being shown throughout our country because of something that was so devastating. I saw a nation demonstrating love for its citizens. This tragedy was not experienced by just one nationality of people, but people from all walks of life, and various countries and businesses were affected.

It was such a sight to witness the love that was being exemplified through the people, coming together in love for one common cause, and that is the security of our homeland. This demonstration of love seemingly lasted for a good while.

We thank God for our military, other agencies, our law enforcement officers, people praying daily, and those who are daily on their watch looking out for suspicious and unusual things around us to keep our country safe. Thank God, He has helped those whose job is to protect our country to discover and uncover many traps that have been set to try and bring other tragedies to our homeland.

But what happened to the demonstration of love for each other like we experienced during those days? We were having several prayer vigils, coming together as one, praying and fasting, repenting, afraid there were going to be more attacks because of the threats we were receiving. There have been other threats and even devices planted with attempts to cause destruction in our homeland, but thank God He has not allowed any of them to unfold.

But as usual, what do we do after years pass, and we get comfortable once again? We go back to business as usual and forget that we all had just gathered at the altar several years earlier and repented and told God we would show more love toward one another and not go back to our ungodly ways. I know—I can't tell you how many times I've done this. I promised God I would do right at a time when I was in trouble or looking at troubles in my life and all around me, and after a few years of comfort, I found myself slipping back into my old ways.

I know one thing: when I think about the encounter Nate

had after the vision that scared him to his knees, he inquired of God as to why he saw anger. God responded and told him that He was angry because of the hypocrisy in our homeland and He didn't leave anyone out. When God spoke, I began to take inventory of the way I was living and asked God to help me not to be a pretender, pretending to live one way, but on the other hand living another, because to be a hypocrite is to live a lie.

I have to tell this one story that I learned when I was pretending with my father. My father brought us up under really strict Christian guidelines, and one of the things he always taught us was to not be a hypocrite. He said, "If you're not really living a godly Christian life, don't pretend to be." He said to be either in or out, which reminds me of something that God said to us in His Word. He said He wanted us to be either hot or cold, because if we were lukewarm He would spew us out. All God was saying is that He didn't want us to be hypocrites, because hypocrites would not make it to heaven.

But here's my story: I remember something that happened between my father and me that was so funny. My father brought us up not to wear makeup—this was part of the restrictions in our church back in the day. So when I graduated from high school and went off to college and got all grownup and stuff, I decided there was nothing wrong with me wearing a little makeup. However, I always wanted to respect my father when I was around him and not wear makeup. He would really get upset when he saw us with makeup on, especially if we called ourselves a Christian. The other thing is I just didn't want him keying in on me.

So one weekend I decided to go home to visit and still

show some respect to my father. So about fifteen miles away from home, we stopped at a gas station and I decided to take the red nail polish off my nails. When we arrived home, later that evening my dad was working on the plumbing at the kitchen sink and he asked for a tool, and since I was standing next to him, I handed him whatever tool he asked for.

Well, the next morning, my mom had cooked a delicious country breakfast, and we were all sitting around the table talking and my mom just burst out laughing and we wanted to know what she was laughing about. She said when she and my dad went to bed the night before, he was so upset. We asked why and she went on to say that my dad told her that when he was under the kitchen sink and I handed him a tool, he looked down and saw my feet and I had red nail polish on my toes.

I looked down at my toes and saw the red polish, then we all burst out laughing. I told them that when we stopped at the gas station, I remembered to take the polish off my fingernails but forgot about my toenails. I learned from that little episode that when trying to pretend to be one thing and hide it from others, at some point and time there will be a slipup.

From that day forward, I decided that I was going to be the same everywhere I went. It was too much of a headache to try to be a hypocrite. I decided the way I looked at work, at church, or in the supermarket would be the same because God saw me anyway. I am not saying that wearing the nail polish was a sin, but what I am saying is just to be real—don't be a hypocrite about it. If I didn't believe that wearing the polish was going to put me in hell or cause me not to go to heaven, I should not have been trying to hide it. Trust me, it was not the nail polish that was making me live a sinful lifestyle; the sin was definitely coming from my heart and not the polish. It was those other ungodly things that God wasn't pleased with.

God sees our hearts, and our ways are before Him every second of the day. There are some things that we do that He is not pleased with, and He will let us know that He sees what we are doing and how we are living. We can't hide it from Him.

God provides us with answers through messages, but many times we don't want to accept His answers. We may never understand why 9/11 had to happen the way it did, but we must continue to pray and ask God to help us love and trust Him and show love toward one another.

Now, the question for me is, the next time I see such a disaster in a dream, will I share it with others, other than my husband and my sister? What will I do differently from what I have done in the past, now that I know it is God who reveals such things to me? I have learned to seek for more information concerning what God shows me and not make light of it or forget about it, but inquire of Him as to what's going on. I will find out if He wants me to respond, when He wants me to respond, or whom He wants me to inform.

Maybe God has revealed something catastrophic to you that may be going to happen in the future. Are you inquiring of Him, asking Him any questions, such as, whether it is inevitable, how to be prepared, how to relay the message, who to relate the message to, and when to relay the message? There are so many questions to ask when we see such devastating events, but all too often we just sit and wonder what in the world we just saw. However, if we seek God diligently

and earnestly for answers to what we saw, He just might en-
lighten us and give us more specifics, but it also means that
we must be willing to listen and accept the message He's conveying.

13

The Interpreter

Several people have dreams, but what I've noticed is that many times people don't have a clue as to what their dreams mean. For example, who would have thought that the dream Nate had when he saw beasts flying toward buildings and landing on top of them represented airplanes? Well, I believe if we would have shared his dream with some other people and these people decided to get a group of dream interpretation experts together to try to determine what in the world Nate had seen, the meeting may have gone like this:

This group could include psychologists, doctors, dream interpreters, artists, computer animators, and whoever else the people who called the meeting would have included that they thought could be of assistance in interpreting his dream.

So now the minds go to work and the artist or computer animator starts drawing as Nate describes to the group what he actually saw. Let's start with the scenario where Nate was running down the street and looked up and saw two very tall buildings that reached into the sky, and he noticed one of them had some sort of an object on the top of the building. Beginning from this point, since we now have a visual aid, more than likely someone would have pointed out that the object was an antenna.

As Nate begins to describe the beasts he saw flying to the top of the buildings, we would have discovered the only way beasts can fly is that they had to have wings. Let's just consider that most of the beasts Nate saw, if it was in real life, would not have wings. We continued to name other animals that have wings, other than birds and bats that could possibly fly to the top of a building. Certainly there may have been other animals that had wings in ancient times that could fly at such height but not in this day and time. However, I'm willing to believe that someone would have thought about other things that fly, such as helicopters and airplanes, because we do sometimes refer to airplanes as "birds"; so let's just say the computer animator would have drawn airplanes flying to the buildings.

Now at this point Nate tells the group that he then saw the beasts drop something on top of the buildings, but he couldn't recognize what it was, all he knows is that each beast dropped something on both buildings and he describes it as best as he could, so the computer animator draws up something that resembles what Nate saw and shows it being dropped on the buildings. Then he tells them he was running down the street, and he happened to look back toward the buildings and saw one building falling down and later the other one, and the computer animator completes the dream in animation.

So now they will do a recap of what the animator came up with so far and try to get an understanding of what may be going on in Nate's dream using the group's interpretation—airplanes flying on top of two buildings and dropping something and buildings falling; then they look at each other and say, "What in the world?"

With all the details, as much as what Nate saw, and the clues given to the animator, after everyone takes a look at this dream on the screen and reviews it several times, I'm willing to believe that someone would have come up with the understanding that Nate possibly could have dreamed that he saw airplanes flying on top of two very tall buildings and those airplanes dropping something that would have attributed to the buildings being destroyed.

Now that it's been drawn out, and we were able to get more insight on Nate's dream, the group may come up with the answer of what happened to the buildings. However, there would be more questions. Who would be responsible for such an attack? What city could it be? What country? What date could this tragedy occur? What time of the day? Nate didn't see any people in the dream, except for himself, but let's say the question comes up of whether there were any people there surrounding the buildings. The most important concern should be, how can it be stopped, can it be stopped at all, or is it inevitable?

There can be many things to learn from a dream, and this is the reason that I've learned to pray and ask God for understanding and interpretation of the dreams that He gives to me and others. We can call for all the experts we believe can help us come up with the true interpretation; however, when it's God revealing something through a dream or giving us a message, God and only God can give us the understanding and true meaning of the entire matter.

Sometimes, just as in Nate's dream, yes, we can piece some of the puzzle together to determine what was going to happen, but did these images help determine who was really behind it? Could the group of experts have been able to determine the city and date it was going to happen? In this scenario that I described, these questions were not answered. However, there was enough information for someone to take it and work on it to investigate and determine how this could possibly happen, how it could get to the point of the airplanes flying to the buildings and the buildings being destroyed.

Then there are other dreams that even the best artists, computer animators, and dream interpretation experts brought together would not be able to put two and two together and come up with the correct understanding because we don't have either enough clues or a clue as to what the dreamer saw. No matter what was described to them and what was drawn out, nothing adds up; therefore, we need more insight.

For example, God showed me the latter part of what happened on the attack of 9/11, when I saw people running, crying, and screaming for help and covered with dust and debris flying all in the streets. If I were in a meeting with a group of experts who were brought in to interpret the dream and I described everything I saw in the dream, would we have come up with an attack of any sort, or would we have thought it had something to do with the weather?

Let's say the artist or animator was there to provide us with some visual aid, and as I described to them what I saw, it appeared that the event that took place in the dream just didn't include enough information. There were not enough clues as there were in Nate's dream. At least with his dream, there were some clues that we could use. In Nate's dream the beasts, or airplanes (if we decided to go with the planes), had destroyed the buildings. However, in my dream you can see none of what caused the people's reactions to the chaos nor what caused the dust and debris, therefore, we don't have a clue as to what they were running from, besides a cloud of dust. What I saw in my dream was the aftereffects of something devastating that had happened. So here we have people running covered with dust, some with briefcases in their hands, and as they were running they were also looking back at whatever was going on.

These could be some of the questions concerning this dream: What city was it in? One thing I did notice is that it was in the daytime. What was going on? I didn't know because I didn't see that part in the dream. This is one of those dreams where you had no clue as to what was happening, so how would the group go about trying to interpret what my dream meant? However, as I previously mentioned in the chapter on 9/11, as I sat down with my eyes glued to the television screen, I saw a flash of what I saw in the dream in 1995 and God spoke to me and told me that was what I had seen, and this was the interpretation of what I saw in that dream.

Sometimes God will give us more details than at other times. Sometimes some dreams are very clear-cut, with no questions to ask and no need for further clarification; however, it does not take away the fact that we still should pray to get God's total message about what He is revealing to us because there is always more to a dream than meets the eye. God already knows all the answers to any questions or concerns that we have about dreams and visions, and He can save us a lot of time and money and give us the true answers because He sees it all from beginning to the end.

In the Bible story of Joseph in Egypt, Joseph gave us the answer to who should interpret dreams: interpretations belong to God, which means that we should seek God and God only for the interpretation and understanding of any dream that He shows us. We have to remember to do as Joseph did when Pharaoh heard that he could interpret dreams and he told Joseph his dream. Joseph quickly corrected him and told him that it was not he who was interpreting the dream, but it was God who was speaking through him who would provide the interpretation and give understanding of what Pharaoh dreamed.

When Joseph told Pharaoh what his dreams meant, God did not only tell Pharaoh what He was about to do, but He also gave him instructions of what to do before the famine came. Now this is one reason I believe it's very important to seek God for interpretation and understanding. As demonstrated in the story about Pharaoh and Joseph, God will not only give us the understanding of the dream, but there's always more. He will tell us what to do, how to respond, and what actions to take. God gave Pharaoh some bad news that a famine was coming to their land; however, at the same time He provided him with some good news and wisdom of how his people could be spared and not perish. He gave them instructions on what to do to get them through the famine.

God told Pharaoh that he needed to appoint officers over the land, so Pharaoh chose Joseph to be over the officers because Pharaoh said that God had given Joseph the interpretation of what was to come upon the land. Pharaoh told him that there was no one as discerning and wise as he was. Pharaoh had also noticed before he put Joseph in prison that everything Joseph put his hand to do prospered. God had given Joseph the interpretation of what was to come upon the entire world, and Pharaoh made Joseph ruler over Egypt. Even though there was a famine in the entire world, God had prepared Egypt for hard times, and they survived (Genesis 41).

I've always been told that if God shows me something in a dream and the same dream is repeated frequently (for instance, I keep dreaming about the same thing, maybe twice in one day, like Pharaoh did), or if I keep having the same dream within a short period of time over and over again, it could be that whatever I've been seeing is about to happen soon.

Therefore I know I had better get to praying and perhaps sharing it with whomever God wants me to share it with, to get an understanding about what's getting ready to happen and find out from God how to respond, if there's any action that must be taken, any preparation that we need to take, and any other communication that need to be conveyed and how to convey it.

Notice, before Pharaoh called for Joseph, he had previously called for other dream interpreter experts, but none of them could interpret his dream. However, since the dream was something God was going to allow to happen, the only person to whom He gave the understanding of Pharaoh's dream was Joseph.

There are times when God does let us know the understanding of a dream, but all too many times we just ignore it. There are certain dreams that it's best not to ignore.

There are some dreams that no matter how we try and guess, assume, figure out, use computer animators, and any other methods to interpret dreams that God will not allow anyone to get the interpretation but the person He wants to give it to, and He allows that person to relay the message so people will know that God gave the interpretation.

Also, as far as ungodly dreams, it's important to pray and ask God to keep them from entering into our heads when we are sleeping. If the ungodly dreams come into our sleep that would only mean that the one who is causing the ungodly dream is an ungodly spirit. When we wake up from that ungodly dream, the same spirit will continue to try to make us act upon those things we dreamed about. If we are not strong, we may entertain those dreams or try and make that dream come true, not realizing that there will be unfavorable consequences to come for responding or acting upon the ungodly dreams.

God does not bring ungodly dreams into our sleep. Therefore, when there is any doubt if a dream is from God, ask Him. We should not be afraid to ask God if a dream is from Him. It's very important to seek God for interpretation, understanding, and clarification concerning the message that He gives us through the dream or vision because He doesn't want us to be deceived.

14

What Happened to the Prophetic Dreams?

If you have experienced dreams that come true, whether occasionally or quite frequently, maybe there was a period or point in your life when it seemed as if those types of dreams went away. You noticed you had not had them in a while. I've been there, and it wasn't that I wasn't having dreams at all, because I had dreams but they were not the ones where I knew that God was communicating something to me. I don't want anyone to think that I think every dream that I have is from God. Trust me—they're not. I wanted to clear this up because I have had some of those other dreams too.

Every now and then I have dreams, and I don't have to ask God if it was from Him or the devil. The dream was quite blatant—no questions asked. When I woke up, I knew that dream wasn't from God; therefore, I've learned to always pray and ask God to not let me have those ungodly dreams.

This is the very reason we must be so careful of the things that we let enter into our minds, whether it's from the television, at the movie theater, listening to certain songs or music, and even reading certain books. Sometimes those things will stay embedded in the back of our minds subconsciously, and we may dream about them.

There was a period in my life when it seemed that I quit having what we call prophetic dreams. They are prophetic because there were definitely messages being conveyed from God, and many of the things I dreamt came true. As you have read earlier, I had dreams about things and within months, weeks, and even days they would happen.

As I look back on that period in my life when I noticed that I wasn't having these dreams, I wondered what happened. I wondered if I would ever have them again. I knew that God was showing me things, so I wondered if God had left me. This was during a period when I had stopped going to church, stopped spending a lot of time in God's Word, and I had gotten distracted with other things that did not include seeking the way God wanted me to live. Therefore it appeared I had left Him, but He didn't leave me.

Why in the world would I walk away from God who had been showing me so many things? He would not only speak with me in dreams, but sometimes He would talk directly to me. But I let life's distractions take me in another direction that was not pleasing to Him, and I allowed these things to lure me away from going to the house of God, away from reading His Word, and sometimes away from being in the company of godly people.

One day as I sat thinking about my past and some of the dreams I used to have, I noticed I had not had a prophetic dream in a while. Then I prayed and said, "Oh, God, please don't take the dreams from me." I began to ask God to forgive me and take me back to the place where He would often communicate with me in dreams. I asked Him to take me back into His loving arms that I had walked away from.

I remember once when I had walked away from God, I dreamt that I had been left down here on earth, and God had come and taken His people to heaven. I will never forget that day. I woke up frightened, and I ran outside and looked around. It seemed like the entire world was quiet, and no one was to be found. I ran back inside the house and called my sister. I figured if she were home, I was safe; and it was just a dream or what some of us call a nightmare even though it was in the daytime. However, when she didn't answer, I really got scared. It was a few minutes later when I discovered it was just a dream, but this really got my attention. I began to repent to God and told Him I didn't want to be left behind.

I then realized that God was watching over me the entire time when I wanted to go another direction and do my own thing. I realized that He had His arms outstretched all the time, waiting for me to come back home to Him so He could communicate with me the way He used to. He was there all the time, waiting on me to come back to Him. God wants to speak to us, and He has various ways of doing so. I believe when that time comes and God speaks, He will let us know if it's Him. I am so grateful that God had mercy on me and showed His love toward me. I had the dream about Him coming back for His church before it really happened. It showed me that God cared about where I was headed, which was down the wrong highway, and it allowed me an opportunity to get back on the right one.

You know, God didn't have to let me have that dream that frightened me so, but He knew it would get my attention. I definitely would have still been doing what I wanted to do, continuing to go down the wrong pathway of life. However, one thing I have noticed is now that I seek to be closer to God and learn more about how He wants me to live in this world, I am having more of the prophetic dreams. God is using these dreams to direct me to pray for others and about certain situations.

I am so glad that God opened up my understanding as to why He communicates to me in dreams in such a way. I know many people have dreams. There may be people who are experiencing or have experienced these dreams, who may not even acknowledge God as the Father or Jesus Christ as their Lord and Savior, but I am willing to believe that if you ask the Father, "Is it You revealing these dreams to me?" He will answer. God knows our hearts, and He knows if we are sincere in our asking, therefore, I believe He'll let you know if it was Him or not. God is not the author of confusion; He does not want us to live a confused life.

As a young person, I didn't know what was going on with these dreams. I didn't realize that God was trying to communicate with me, and I definitely didn't recognize the love He had for me. But I can say that God had His ways of drawing me near to Him, and I am so glad that I took notice, listened, and obeyed when He spoke and got me back on the right pathway.

What happened to the prophetic dreams at the time period in my life when it appeared that they had disappeared? The answer is, the dreams were always there and God was always there, but I just wasn't in the right place nor the position spiritually to receive them because I was too busy trying to go my own way and do my own thing. I am willing to believe that God was revealing them to others because He speaks to many people in prophetic dreams; I was just missing out, but the dreams were still going forth.

God speaks to us because He cares about us. He is concerned about what we do, where we are headed, and the decisions we make in this life. I have learned to get connected to people who love God and love to spend time with Him in prayer because those are the people who have a really close relationship with Him. They seem to be so sensitive to His Spirit and know that, "Yes, He's speaking." Why? Because they listen as He speaks, they talk to Him quite often, and they know His voice. It's the quality time that we spend with God that makes the difference.

15

It's a "God Thing"

Now that we understand that the things we see (the motion pictures) in our dreams may sometimes be God conveying messages to us; we also understand that dreams can be a method that God uses to communicate—it's a "God Thing." If we believe it is a God Thing, we can take more notice of what we are seeing and more time to communicate with the dream giver—God Himself.

I believe many people, just in casual conversations, share dreams with one another because sometimes dreams appear to have some sort of meaning. We feel as if there could be some sort of message; therefore, we say, "You know I had this really strange dream last night."

It could be the same as in the case of the baker and the butler, who both had dreams. Joseph saw the countenance on their faces and asked them why they looked so sad (Genesis 40:1-8). You could be in the presence of someone who saw this puzzling and wearisome countenance on your face and asked, "Hey, what's wrong? You seem disturbed about something. Is there anything bothering you?" Your reply may be,

"Well, by the way there is. I had this dream last night, and I wonder if it means anything." The person asks you if you would like to share the dream, and when you do, they may say that God can give the interpretation and they go on to interpret as God gives the answer to them.

You may have never even thought of God while trying to figure out what you saw. On the other hand, you may have woken up and asked Him, "God, what did I just see?" to find out later that there was a message in the dream.

I really do believe there are many people whom God speaks to through dreams, but they don't always realize that it is Him. When we fail to realize that it could be God, we don't pay attention to the dream, and when we don't pay attention to the dream, we can miss out on receiving pertinent information. I've had to learn to ask God to help me to know when it's Him, because there are also many deceiving spirits and deceiving dreams that may seem like they are from Him, but they are not. It is very important that we understand this, so we won't be deceived.

God wants us to ask and inquire of Him. He does not want us to live in darkness. He will open up our eyes that we may see clearly and our understanding that we may understand the messages that are being conveyed to us through dreams.

Too many times we run to the wrong resources and will more than likely get the wrong interpretation, if we get one at all. We share it with too many people, and they respond by telling us what they *think* we saw in the dream, without consulting God. God does have people whom He uses to interpret dreams, and we should seek God to lead us to them. Many times God will speak directly to us and give us the interpretation, if we are paying attention.

I'm glad God uses our grandfathers and grandmothers, schoolteachers, fathers and mothers, other relatives, neighbors, His ministers, that stranger that just walked up to us, and others whom He has given the gift to interpret dreams, to give us a clearer understanding of the messages He wants to receive.

Isn't it good that God will show us a dream or vision and even quietly speak to us and say, "Pray for him or her because of My precious love for them?" I've learned that many times people in the Bible days would spend days before God, praying and asking Him for interpretation of dreams, because they knew that if the dream was from God, He would reveal its full meaning.

I've learned that some people covet the gift of dreams or dream interpretation, but sometimes these gifts can bring much grief in our hearts, such as it did for Daniel when he saw a certain vision (Daniel 10). God actually had to send an angel to him to comfort him. Sometimes we don't want to deliver what may sound like unfavorable messages to our close friends or loved ones, or to anyone for that matter. Yes, this can be a tough responsibility, because not all dreams appear to be favorable. However, when we ask a man or woman of God to interpret a dream, the interpreter cannot afford to water down whatever God speaks to them because they don't want to be the bearer of bad news; whatever God gives us we have to reveal.

It is such a blessing for God to communicate to us in such a way. God knows everything. He already knows the things that have not come to pass but will in the future. Sometimes if it's concerning our safety, He will give us a way of escape and protect us from harm that could come our way, if we seek Him for guidance. Sometimes He will reveal who our enemies are. He knows how to stop our enemies from destroying us. He will keep us through a Great Recession and show us how to survive. He can give us instructions on how to better secure our school campuses. He will heal our minds when it seems like things are so hectic surrounding us, and we can't seem to hold it together. He will protect us from contaminated foods, liquids, and other products, and not allow them to harm or destroy us.

It's a God Thing. It is so important that we ask God to teach us how to hear Him when He is speaking to us. It's so important that we seek God for spiritual guidance, to be led by His Holy Spirit through life's dilemmas and life's issues and to allow Him to teach us how to live according to His will and way. There are messages for all of us in those dreams and visions. We must listen and pay close attention as He gives us understanding and clarification of what He is revealing and, most of all, how we are to respond. When God speaks to us, we are held accountable to do something.

Other Books You May Be Interested In

God Wants to Speak by Nathan Scott
God wants to let us know that He has always been, and still is, in control. He continues to use prophets to relay His messages to people, whether for correction, blessings, or warnings. Beyond the prophets, God also desires intimacy with each of us by speaking to us directly, or through dreams and visions. In this book the author encourages us to take a closer look at these messages to see just how much love God has for His people.
ISBN 978-1-58169-326-3, 133 PG. PB $11.99

Intimacy With God by Nathan Scott
The Bible is given to us to instruct, rebuke, guide, and teach us God's heart and mind concerning our lives, and its hidden truths are attainable. But sometimes our efforts to understand its truths fail, and we're left without the answers we need. It is through an intimate relationship with God in Jesus Christ, that we are able to access the knowledge and wisdom contained within it.
ISBN 978-1-58169-248-8   96PG. PB $8.99

If you would like to contact Nathan for a speaking engagement, an appearance or to obtain his books, please visit www.blesscott.com for contact information or write to:

Nathan Scott
P. O. Box 530634
Grand Prairie, TX. 75053
www.blesscott.com

About the Author

Marilyn serves in the ministry with her husband, Nathan Scott, who is an ordained minister and author. She is known as a praying woman who exercises the gift of prophetic dreams and intercessory prayer. Marilyn traveled with and was mentored by a nationally known evangelist whom she was also an armor bearer to while conducting prayer revivals. Marilyn has twenty years experiences working in corporate America as an inside client representative, sales specialist, retiree coordinator, benefits specialist, and reservation agent. Marilyn and Nathan are parents, grandparents, and great-grandparents.

If you would like to contact Marilyn for a speaking engagement, an appearance or to obtain more books, please visit www.blesscott.com for contact information or write to:

Marilyn Scott
P. O. Box 530634
Grand Prairie, TX. 75053

CPSIA information can be obtained at www.ICGtesting.com
Printed in the USA
LVOW040345100712

289402LV00001B/9/P